FOR THE AUDIENCE OF ONE

For the Audience of One

The Soul Survivor Guide
to Worship

Mike Pilavachi with Craig Borlase

Hodder & Stoughton
LONDON SYDNEY AUCKLAND

First published in Great Britain 1999

10 9 8 7 6 5 4 3 2 1

British Library Cataloguing in Publication Data
A record for this book is available from the British Library

ISBN 0 340 72190 1

Typeset by Hewer Text Ltd, Edinburgh
Printed and bound in Great Britain by
Clays Ltd, St Ives PLC

Hodder and Stoughton Ltd
A Division of Hodder Headline PLC
338 Euston Road
London NW1 3BH

To Matt and Beth Redman,
Worship and Evangelism, a great partnership

Contents

Acknowledgments

We would like to thank a number of our friends who have helped us in the writing of this book: David Moloney at Hodder & Stoughton for his encouragement and patience as each new deadline came and went; Emma Mitchell for efficiently typing the transcripts; Rev. Dr Mark Stibbe for rescuing us from many theological disasters and Matt Redman for his many wise and helpful comments. We recruited a small army to read through the manuscript for any mistakes and we hope they did a thorough job! They include: David Seddon, Ellie Harding, Neil Pearce, Verity Furneaux, Tim Hughes, Martyn Layzell, Liz and Sarah Redman, Dennis and Miriam Layzell, and Carole Japhtha. Also, we must thank Taryn Bibby who, as Mike's PA, has contributed beyond the call of duty, and Jon Stevens, whose servant heart and commitment to the cause have been inspiring. Finally, thanks to Bishop David and Mary Pytches for starting us off on our little adventure and all the team at Soul Survivor for being you and staying here!

Introduction

A dynamic occurs when people worship God that you won't find anywhere else on the face of this earth. Worship is about God, worship is for God, and worship is to God. But for some wonderful reason, when we try and give something back to God, so often we end up receiving from him.

Indeed, worshipping God can usher in all sorts of 'benefits' for us – an uplifting sense of God's presence, emotional healing, all sorts of signs and wonders, and even salvation. It's because of these wonderful blessings that we need to keep reminding ourselves constantly that worship is 'all about Jesus'. It's not about what we can get out of it; we don't invest to yield a good return. Worship is for God's pleasure and glory. The title of Mike and Craig's book says it all – *For the Audience of One*.

At Soul Survivor we've been on a journey of discovery with the whole worship thing. It's always been 'the' thing as far as we're concerned. Everything else flows from that place of relationship with God. While worship obviously concerns the whole of our lives, when we come together, music can be a particularly beautiful expression of it. We started discovering this in a number of ways. Mike, for example, spent his early Christian years heavily impressed by the worship songs of the Fisherfolk. Having played me the worn out tapes twenty years down the road it's sometimes a little difficult to comprehend his obsession fully! But the point is, the Fisherfolk were one of the groups that ushered in the rediscovery of the dynamic that occurs when we pour out our love to God through music.

More than anywhere else, we've learnt our worship values from the Vineyard. I first encountered this brand of intimate, passionate worship at the age of seven, two months after my dad had died, and it had a huge impact on me. Since then I have grown up with the wonderful reality that the fearsome Almighty God would beckon even me with his hand of friendship. This, to me, through the window of the cross, is the mystery of the universe.

It was in 1989 that we started, with a small group of others, to give over an occasional evening just to worship God and pursue this mystery. We only had the bare essentials – a nearly in-tune acoustic guitar and our voices. If you'd have heard Mike's voice and my guitar playing, you probably wouldn't have stuck around for long, but fortunately for us we knew it wasn't about that! Time after time, when we sought to bring our songs of adoration to God, we'd find ourselves caught up in his amazing presence.

Since those days we've read loads of books on worship, heard loads of talks and had loads of practice, but in the end I know that if we don't still have the same heart for worship we had back then, we won't have progressed anywhere. There was a raw, simple passion to bring our love songs to God, and draw near to him. They were special times, and I sometimes match my heart against them now and wonder if for all my supposed 'experience' I still have the same heart.

This book itself looks at many ways we can learn more about worship and, indeed, become better worshippers, but in the end reminding us there's no substitute for having a heart of worship. What exactly is that? For me, it's summed up nowhere better than in Ephesians 5:10: 'Find out what pleases the Lord.' That's the heart of worship – to want to discover the actions, attitudes and ways that are going to make God's heart glad. I think, at least I hope, this is what has spurred us on to try and discover more about worship – a desire to delight the heart of God with our offerings.

It's definitely an exciting time to be alive. We've had the privilege of being involved in Soul Survivor, and also travelling round a bit getting a glimpse of what God is doing. Everywhere we've been we've witnessed the same thing – a passionate church, ready to worship God with everything within them. It's far deeper than any music could ever go – these worshippers are 'serious' about taking up the challenge of spending the whole of their lives upon Jesus.

In a sense, this book is the story of where Soul Survivor's at, in terms of worship. Some of it has been shaped in various meetings and conferences around the place. Lots of it has been learnt both the hard and easy way at Soul Survivor Watford, the church we belong to and Mike pastors. Loads of it the old Greek has formulated inside his own head, with the essential aid of his Bible.

For the Audience of One

The book does a great job of coming at worship from all sorts of angles. When Mike speaks on worship, he has a real gift of making the subject accessible and entertaining, yet challenging and bringing the point home. With Craig's help this gift translates brilliantly into writing. I've hung around Pilavachi for a long time now, and learnt a load about worship from him. Read this book and you'll find out effort-free everything it's taken me ten years to get out of him!

But in the end, this is not just a book about worship. It is a manual that will help the reader discover more of what pleases the heart of God, and lead us right to the very heart of worship. Enjoy.

Matt Redman
February 1999

Preface

This whole book is about worship. It is written because my friends and I at Soul Survivor believe that the adoration of God is the highest calling and top priority for every Christian. In this book I have tried to tell some of the things we have learned about worship (often through painful experience). However, if you're standing in a shop and don't want to pay for this book, the following will go some way to explaining why we are so passionate about the worship of God.

This book is written because I believe the Bible says that worship is the reason for our existence. This book is also written because, as I have encountered him in worship, Jesus has changed and healed me. I remember in 1983 when John Wimber put on his first conference at Westminster Central Hall, I had just arrived at St Andrew's, Chorleywood, the church that would be my home for the next seventeen years and beyond. I'd been a deacon of a Baptist church in Harrow and everything that could have gone wrong did. From relationships to work, it seemed like my life was a disaster-zone. I left the church completely broken, thinking that I was never going to be happy.

As I joined St Andrew's I heard about the conference that John Wimber was hosting. I went along and was blown away by it all. He was funny and his teaching was brilliant. I had never heard anything like it before and the ministry times were amazing. There were many new things to experience, but what stood out most was the worship; it totally unhinged me. I spent a whole part of the week just crying and snuffling my way through songs like 'Isn't He Beautiful?' and 'Hold Me, Lord, In Your Arms'. Many of the songs were incredibly simple and yet totally intimate. As I worshipped I found healing for my soul. Intimacy set me free. Finally I had found a way of expressing a relationship with God where I could feed on the truths that I desperately needed to hear. God loved me. He forgave me. He liked me. As I drank it all in I began to want more, as if it had awoken a thirst deep within.

Since then, gradually, I have been finding my healing in that place. I have also found power there – for intercession as well as healing. One of the biggest surprises and joys has been to discover that worship is an incredibly effective evangelistic tool. Over the last few years we have seen thousands of young people come to faith in Jesus as they have found themselves in the midst of a group of passionate worshippers. But most of all I worship because he deserves it. It is the language of our relationship with God. Worship is the highest priority.

1

The Highest Priority

Whichever way you look at it, you cannot alter our highest priority. Try as hard as you like, but you'll never twist the definition of our purpose on earth to read 'I am here to shop' or 'I exist to make money.' Sure, shopping and making a living are part of the fabric of our lives, but they can never be the main reason that we are here. That place is reserved for something special: worship.

Worship is the highest priority of the human race. It is what we were created for and it is why we are here. Worship is our defining characteristic. The big question throughout our history has never been 'will we worship?', instead the issue has always focused on 'what will we worship?' Think about it: we all worship. Hindus worship, Buddhists worship, Muslims worship, materialists worship, Marxists worship, Conservatives worship, even Arsenal supporters worship. This has been true for centuries, and it provides much common ground between ourselves and that cast of thousands we read so much about in the Bible, the Israelites. Throughout their history, as depicted in the Old Testament, if they didn't worship the Lord their God, they very soon found other things to worship.

1

But things don't just stop there. Not only has God made it our highest priority, but he has also called us to a lifestyle of worship, to be at it round the clock. Does that mean that we are never without our Walkman pumping in inspirational praise and worship tunes? Thankfully not, as God has a bigger idea of what he wants from us. Jesus said in Mark 12:29–31 that the greatest commandment in the whole law is that we love the Lord our God with all our heart, soul, mind and strength. That is a commandment to worship. To love the Lord our God with all that we have is to develop and maintain an intimate relationship with our Maker. That's what God wants.

My background is the Anglican Church; I've been working within it for years – actually, that's not entirely true, as I was a Baptist for quite a while. That all ended when my enterprises as the leader of an open youth group ended in chaos, destruction and the use of all three emergency services. There are some aspects of the Anglican liturgy that I love because they are so rich. The prayer of thanksgiving, which we say when we break the bread, points out that 'it is our duty and our joy, at all times and in all places to give [God] thanks and praise, holy Father, heavenly King, almighty and eternal God'.

Sometimes thanking God seems a little removed from the more obvious expressions of joy – when did you last hear of drugs that made you feel thankful all over? Sometimes it may feel more like duty than joy, but it is our duty and joy. Throughout the centuries this point has been stressed by Bible teachers from the Old Testament until today. While reading up for this book, I came across a quote from Graham Kendrick, who suggested that, if we really worshipped as we should, there wouldn't be any need for evangelism. The prospect of an evangelism-free life could have you pounding the wall either with rage or delight. The point is, that if we really worshipped as we should, if we loved God as we will love him in heaven, our worship would be so inspiring that people would flock to where we are.

Richard Foster, in his book *Celebration of Discipline* (Hodder & Stoughton), says that 'the divine priority is this; worship first, service second'. When we commit ourselves first and foremost to worshipping God as he deserves, then the acts of service will follow. Put another way, God desires intimacy with us first and foremost. Put yet another way: remember Mary and Martha (see Luke 10:38–42)? Which one did Jesus commend? In other words, 'when God has our hearts, our hands will surely follow'!

A Definition of Worship

This all might be getting a little out of hand, moving on too fast. Perhaps it would be a good time to get back to basics and find out exactly what worship is. Put simply, it is to give God what is rightfully his. And what does the Creator of the universe deserve? How about adoration, praise, thanks and love? Those are a few of the things that he is worth, and they help define the way that we should be relating to him.

Another defining characteristic of worship is that it must come before everything else. That doesn't mean that we ought to have our ears permanently clamped between two Kendrick-blaring headphones. What it means is that we need to have our hearts right. If we are first of all lovers of God, people who are devoted to praising and worshipping him, then our deeds will be powered by the right motives. When we get our priorities right and put the worship of God first, then everything else falls into place. When we put other things first – even other good things, other good, Christian things – then everything falls apart. It's as simple as that. St Augustine (a very ancient bloke) had a good phrase. He said: 'Love God and do what you like.' By that he meant that when we truly love him then we will want to do the things that please him.

At Soul Survivor we've believed from the beginning that our first calling is to be worshippers of God. When the people of Israel turned away and replaced God with idols, everything fell apart. We are trying to avoid that particular trap by making God the central focus of our lives.

We were created to worship God, we were made with a yearning for intimacy with our Maker. He made us in his image so that we could have relationship with him. When, for whatever reason, we turn from God, we will always try to replace him with something else. Our God-substitute could be anything, from sex to ambition to other religious figures. What is for sure though, is that whenever the Israelites took time out from God, they ended up in a terrible state: sick, fighting, hating, splitting. When they went back to God, things were better. Relationship with God is the heart's true home.

In Jeremiah 2:13 the prophet proclaims the following words: 'My people have committed two sins: They have forsaken me, the spring of living water, and have dug their own cisterns, broken cisterns that cannot hold water.' If we forsake God, the spring of living water, then we try to find our own water; we dig our own cisterns. This is a helpful picture as it shows God as a life source, a vital component to our survival. When we ignore him, we find other things to be our life source. The trouble is, that you have to go a pretty long way to beat the 'spring of living water', that's some liquid. Tapping into the substandard and the impure guarantees us nothing but trouble. We find eventually that all our God-substitutes are like broken cisterns. They don't hold water and cannot quench our thirst.

Often the things that we try to squeeze satisfaction out of are all well and good when in their rightful place, but their rightful place is where they need to stay. For example, how on earth could football/shopping/promotion ever be a main purpose in life? Even clubbing together to form a syndicate they seem pale and narrow in comparison to God's great richness and diversity. No, we were made by God, for God. He gave us plenty of toys, but he only ever gave us one purpose.

My Story

Since I've been a Christian God has healed me of many things, but perhaps the most amazing was my tendency towards possessiveness. This was something I had to get healed of when I first became a Christian. My background contains a fair amount of brokenness, and because of that I used to get possessive about people, believing that they didn't like me and would leave at any time. It was a fear that drove me, and I can point to things that happened when I was very young and find its roots.

When I was five and it was time for me to go to school I had my first shock. I hadn't mixed with any other kids until then, and did not have any English-speaking friends. Consequently I could only speak Greek at the time, and I can still remember my first day at school. I can see myself sat on my bed and my mum tying up my shoelaces, putting these strange clothes on me and then taking me to school. I remember the tension that had been building up in the house, and how when I arrived at school all the other kids seemed so much bigger than I was. The screaming and shouting in the playground frightened me. I was unable to understand what was going on.

For months, because I couldn't speak their language I was crippled by shyness. I couldn't communicate and all I did during the breaks was walk up and down the playground on my own. I was scared of all the other pupils. They would play football and I would long to join in but I couldn't, I just didn't know how. Years later, as I started to make relationships, those feelings of being isolated, of being different and of being alone resurfaced whenever I made new friends. I would do anything to keep them, and was in what seemed like a perpetual state of panic. If I saw any of my friends getting on well with anyone else something inside me would knot up and I would panic, feeling convinced that they didn't care about me and would soon be off. I felt as though other people always understood each other better than I could, that they were much happier without me and that I was destined to feel like an outsider for the rest of my life.

I developed a safety strategy that meant I wouldn't ever get hurt: if I felt that someone was about to reject me, I would reject them first. I would withdraw and punish them with my silence. At one point I went for two years without speaking to anyone in my class at school and hardly speaking to anyone in my family. I completely withdrew into myself and was consumed by my inner feelings. My parents didn't know what to do. They tried to get me to talk to my brother and sister but I just couldn't.

It has taken years of finding Jesus as the source of my life to move on from those feelings. I feel like I am the living embodiment of the phrase 'broken cisterns' – I know that on my own I simply would not have made it this far. Finding Jesus meant finding life, although it didn't mean getting fixed immediately. Even now, while I have come so far, I am still vulnerable to some watered-down versions of those old feelings. The test is always what I choose to do when they surface: do I turn to God or do I run away? Turning to God means looking to him to affirm me. It means finding him as the spring of living water as I have poured out my heart in the intimacy of worship. It hasn't failed yet.

2

Sacrifice in Worship

Sacrifice. Not the most exciting of concepts. In fact, this whole sacrifice thing is in need of a severe public image overhaul. Right now it's all too drab, mooching around somewhere between 'charitable giving' and releasing your seat to old people on buses. Drop the S-word into a conversation with most people today and the chances are you'll receive a blank stare by way of return. Sacrifice has almost become an irrelevancy. Maybe with a few nips and tucks, a glitzy advertising campaign and some clever product placement we can make it hip. Perhaps not.

You see, sacrifice isn't supposed to be fun. It isn't even supposed to be rewarding; it is most definitely a one-way street. In these days of personal freedom and the right to direct our own lives, one-way streets are most definitely out. So we have a problem on our hands: God likes sacrifice; we don't. Oh dear.

Sacrifice has always been found right at the heart of worship. It is, if you like, one of the spokes of the wheel. It is inextricably linked to that other favourite of ours, obedience. Throughout the Old Testament, we read story after story which detail the many ways in which the Israelites would offer sacrifices to the Lord,

9

obeying his commands to do so. In all but one of the main Hebrew festivals, the sacrifice of lambs, goats, doves, grain or drink was a key part. Those festivals were not a million miles away from the big Rock Festivals we have today; people got together, had a good time, gave away something that they valued – animals in the case of the Hebrew festivals and access to decent sanitation at Glastonbury.

Perhaps the analogy doesn't stretch quite that far, but at least it introduces the point that the Hebrew festivals weren't all necessarily miserable affairs. They existed to continue communication between Creator and created. On some occasions, the focus was the celebration of God's goodness, while on others it would centre on the process of mourning or the act of asking God to intervene in a specific situation. What they all had in common, though, were sacrifice and obedience.

Sacrifice

I love the passage in 2 Chronicles 7. Solomon and the people of Israel had spent years building the temple in Jerusalem, which was going to be the permanent home for their previously mobile altar.

Such an important artefact needed a pretty special home – hence the prolonged building campaign – designed by a pretty special architect. It was God himself who provided Solomon with the plans, detailing everything from the foundations to the furnishings. As Solomon and his builders followed God's specifications, God sent a message to them (and to us today) that worship is always on his terms, and not on ours. If God was ambivalent towards that whole temple concept then he wouldn't have got involved. As it was, he was specific and detailed in his instructions. It's the same with our worship: God likes it and he wants to make sure that we get it right.

That idea seems to conflict with contemporary thought. Today, we subscribe to the belief that worship is a personal choice. If I want to worship God by banging a drum then surely I am free to do so. Likewise, I cannot criticise those who opt for High Church liturgy and structured worship. This is only part of the truth however. Yes, it is wrong for us to try to make others worship on our terms, but that also extends to God; we don't have the last word in the direction of our own worship of God. What we have to do is worship our Maker on his own terms. After all, if the worship is for him then surely we should pause and enquire as to his preferences, his tastes and be a little less consumed with ours. 'Lord, how would you like us to worship you today?' should be the constant question of our hearts.

Before that sets you off in a panic, consider God's infinite size and creativity, as well as the fact that you have been made in his image. The chances are that the terms that he dictates for how you are to worship him will not be totally alien to you. Anyway, the Lord does not seem to be too bothered about whether it is with an organ or a drum, but he is very bothered that it is in Spirit and truth – that is, from the heart.

Back to the story. Once the temple had been built and they had brought the Ark to it, it was time for the dedication. Chapter 7 starts soon after Solomon has prayed an amazing prayer of dedication:

11

When Solomon finished praying, fire came
down from heaven and consumed the burnt
offering and the sacrifices, and the glory of the
Lord filled the temple. The priests could not
enter the temple of the Lord because the glory
of the Lord filled it. When all the Israelites saw
the fire coming down and the glory of the
Lord above the temple, they knelt on the
pavement with their faces to the ground, and
they worshipped and gave thanks to the Lord
saying, 'He is good, his love endures for ever.'
Then the king and all the people offered
sacrifices before the Lord. And King Solomon
offered a sacrifice of twenty-two thousand head
of cattle and a hundred and twenty thousand
sheep and goats. So the king and all the
people dedicated the temple to God. The
priests took their positions, as did the Levites
with the Lord's musical instruments, which
King David had made for praising the Lord
and which were used when he gave thanks
saying, 'His love endures for ever.' Opposite
the Levites, the priests blew their trumpets,
and all the Israelites were standing. (2 Chronicles 7:1–6)

This is some worship session. It tells us so much that a
quick read often misses some of the juiciest bits. The
whole temple project had been carried out on a big
scale. The labour force topped 153,600 men, there was
enough gold inside to sink the *Titanic* and the dedication service didn't disappoint. The king offered a
sacrifice of 22,000 cows and 120,000 sheep and goats.

Can you imagine that? It wasn't even a bring and share barbecue thrown to say thank you to the workers. No, all this meat was, for want of a better word, wasted. They burnt it up and that was that; no nibbles, left-overs or packed-lunches. The size of the sacrifice was so great that it would have had a drastic effect on the economy. According to David, that was a good sign that the sacrifice was worthy – 'Shall I offer to God that which cost me nothing?' he once mused. The answer is of course that he didn't, and neither should we. Worship is meant to cost something. In Solomon's case, it was a significant dent in his treasury.

That leaves us in a bit of a quandary: how well would you be received entering your local church leading an exodus from the local farms? Of course, we know that Jesus's death met our need to find the perfect physical sacrifice, but that leaves us, supposedly, on the giving end of something far less tangible: the sacrifice of our lives. How on earth do you create harmony between today's structures for worship and the concept of extravagant worship? Isn't the avoidance of the latter precisely why church treasurers exist? True, finance can come into it, but it is from our hearts that the first payment should be made.

Back to Solomon, and the glory of the Lord descends. People knelt on the pavement with their faces to the ground and the priests could not perform their duties. They couldn't enter the temple either, as it was so filled with God's presence, his 'Godness'. The timing of this arrival is no coincidence, and is yet another piece of evidence that points towards the conclusion that the glory of God comes in the place of sacrifice.

That is not the only example of the link between God's glory and our sacrifice. When David danced before the Lord, he danced with all his might: 'David was afraid of the Lord that day and said, "How can the ark of the Lord ever come to me?" He was not willing to take the ark of the Lord to be with him in the City of David. Instead, he took it aside, to the house of Obed-Edom the Gittite' (2 Samuel 6:9–10). It remained there for three months and the Lord blessed him and his entire household.

Isn't that interesting? The Ark of the Lord staying at Obed-Edom's place was enough to bless him.

> Now King David was told, 'The Lord has blessed the household of Obed-Edom and everything he has, because of the ark of God.' So David went down and brought up the ark of God from the house of Obed-Edom to the City of David with rejoicing. When those who were carrying the ark of the Lord had taken six steps he sacrificed a bull and a fattened calf. David, wearing a linen ephod, danced before the Lord with all his might, while he and the entire house of Israel brought up the ark of the Lord with shouts and the sound of trumpets. (2 Samuel 6:12–15)

Michal, the daughter of Saul, watched David from the window, despising him in her heart. It's interesting that David dancing before the Lord with all of his might comes after they bring the Ark of the Covenant from Obed-Edom the Gittite's place to Jerusalem. Now we don't know how far away Obed-Edom lived from Jerusalem, but even if it had been only a few miles, the journey would have been something of an epic. You see, it wasn't just a case of hitching up the old Ark and trotting off down the road. The text indicates that 'When those who were carrying the ark of the Lord had taken six steps, he [David] sacrificed a bull and a fattened calf.' It is quite possible that they performed this sacrifice every six steps.

At the beginning it would probably have been great, a regular march 'n' burn. After a while, though, the novelty was bound to have worn off. Not only would the length of time it took have been frustrating, but again, there was the issue of economics: those cattle had to come from somewhere, and coughing up came at a price. Once the journey is over David makes the final sacrifice, stripping down to his linen ephod and dancing before his God.

You can view the history of the Old Testament sacrifices as a warm-up for the life and (sacrificial) death of Jesus. Once he went to the cross, the obligation to offer sacrifices of bulls and goats and lambs in order to earn salvation was done with; Jesus died once and for all, to earn salvation for us. In a sense, that sacrificial system died when Jesus died; he was the ultimate and none could better him. At the same time, in another sense, the sacrificial system didn't end there because we're commanded in the New Testament to offer a sacrifice of praise. In Romans 12:1 Paul says, 'Therefore, I urge you, brothers, in view of God's mercy, to offer your bodies as living sacrifices, holy and pleasing to God – which is your spiritual act of worship.' That's it: it's not lambs, doves or cows now, it's my body. It's your body. It's our bodies, as living sacrifices. Not dead sacrifices that get burnt up, but living sacrifices. That is our spiritual act of worship. This time, however, we do it not to earn God's favour, in an attempt to win God's love and salvation, but as an expression of our love and adoration, as a response to his salvation.

When I remind myself of this, it stirs me up again. I want to give him the lot and hold nothing of myself back. If we have this understanding when taking part in and leading worship, then the bit where we sing our songs takes its proper place. God's glory often comes when we sacrifice. I want to get closer to God, experience more of his glory and be able to give more of myself as a sacrifice so that I can see his glory.

Obedience

Like oddly matched luminous socks, soft-wave perms and biker jackets, the things that get us excited change with the seasons. Recently, we in the Church have had our fair share of chart toppers, ranging from 1995's fancy for tribal worship (remember the sticks?) to the predicted revival that was due to land some time during May 1997. Of late, those hopes have developed into something less specific: a belief that these are important times. We hear from the pulpit that these days are made great by the promise of God's anointing, by his imminent arrival. I don't know what flight he's booked onto, and I'm not one for making predictions, all I do know is that we are in danger of hyping this thing up. Every generation is important, as is each period of time. Bearing in mind all the Gospels have to say about 'the day and the hour unknown', I think it wise (as well as a guaranteed way of avoiding disappointment) not to plan too far ahead. However, if we are still keen on living in exciting times, there is one thing we can do: serve the Lord wholeheartedly. If we do that, then we really will see fireworks.

Before we went all tribal, and long before we marked our year planners with a subtle R for revival, we were talking about what it meant to be radical. As a buzz word it stayed around for a while, and found itself forming the front end of many a motivational phrase: radical lifestyle, radical Christianity, radical worship. At the heart of it all (as with all the things that capture our imagination for a time) was a genuine desire to make a good job of following Jesus.

Looking through the Bible lately, I've been struck by how worship is presented through lifestyle. Read between the lines, and stories reveal a subtext that promotes what I can only describe as radical obedience. The thing is, being radical isn't about the way you sing songs or the kind of tunes you play, being radical is about the life you live. That makes for some serious potential obedience.

I've been to Finland a couple of times, and on both occasions it's done my pride no good whatsoever. I've arrived a confident, slightly quirky international speaker and left a tired, humbled man. I get a little nervous and insecure before going somewhere new. I therefore occupy my mind during the flight over with thoughts such as 'I hope they're not too strange' and 'I wonder if I could say I got lost in customs.' True to form, I encountered things that made me cringe. Watching a slightly balding Fin as he marched around the campsite waving a flag for the duration of the festival, I made a mental note to ban balding flag wavers at Soul Survivor the next year. Perhaps I had a bad encounter with semaphore at sea scouts, but flags and me just don't get on.

My disdain subsided when I found out that his main aim was not to advertise flag waving as a hobby, but to make sure that the event received constant prayer support. He spent hours walking around the site with his flag praying for the meetings. There were others too, praying throughout the night at the back of the hall. Still, I felt that I was on strong ground with my 'cultural relevance' argument. (How many people do you see waving huge flags in Sainsbury's?) Surely our friend must be damaging the festival's public image by making himself (and us) look so 'unique'?

Talking to the guy finished me off. Forget the state of his hair and his flag and his sense of cool, I thought afterwards. I discovered that he is one of the most committed prayer warriors in Scandinavia. If I could have half the dedication he has to following God, I would be a much better Christian. You see, I find it hard to be servant-hearted. When I'm at an event I might be able to sustain the charity for a while, praying with the first couple of people that come up and ask, but after that, I'm out of there.

Having spoken with Mr Flag, I decided to try things his way: servanthood, obedience. I decided that I would say yes to everyone who asked for a chat or prayer. It was just my luck that this happened to be an event that was full of friendly and needy people. They kept on coming: when I had finished speaking, when I was eating, when I was praying for someone else. Instead of getting wound up early on, I managed to stick to my promise and never say no. Forgive me if I slip into Victorious Christian Writer mode here, but I actually did find the whole thing totally, um, liberating. Somehow I managed to gag both my ego and my selfishness and say to myself, 'I'm here to serve you God – would you provide me with the strength?'

I'm not saying we should be constantly dropping out of duties, needs and responsibilities in favour of 'doing the Lord's work'. What I do know is that when I put him first, God taught me a lesson about the kind of radical commitment that forgets about self. This is not meant to be a huge boost for my ego – the plain fact is that this was my first, my only act of radical obedience since my birth. It's actually quite embarrassing, really.

I suppose the first hint towards radical obedience comes in the Sermon on the Mount, where Jesus delivers his manifesto for good living. When he suggested turning the other cheek, going the extra mile and donating the second shirt, he was laying down the law for a new style of life. His metaphors all scream out the instruction to be radical, to live a different way. Doing this shows our obedience to his calling, as well as our love for him: it is worship.

Jesus didn't say, 'If you love me you will sing the latest songs.' What he said was, 'If you love me you will obey my commandments' (John 14:15). There's so much for us to learn from this, and it starts with that prickly little word: obedience. As a youth worker, I suppose I ought to know better than to drop a word like obedience into a book. If there's anything that's bound to turn people off, it's words like obedience. Say it to most people and it will conjure up mental images of fascists, school days and chopped liver. Still, obedience is something we need to get into; it is a biblical principle. As we become slaves to Jesus Christ, we find freedom. It's as servants of God that we find our true selves, and it's in pouring our lives out that we can give our worship. Radical obedience is squaring up to the verse that states, 'If you love me you *will* obey my commandments.' Charles Swindoll wrote this: 'The very best proof of your love for God is obedience – nothing more, nothing less, nothing else.' In my little way when I decided that I was not going to make judgments about who I talked to or who I prayed with, and instead just to be a servant for a while, I found a freedom and a joy from ministering that I hadn't had for ages. Now that's embarrassing to say, but it's the truth. It's also one of the big missing links in the Church today. We struggle when it comes to being a people who will pour ourselves out for our God.

As we're in the mood for dead authors, I might as well drop in a bit of Oswald Chambers. He wrote this: 'How can we talk of making a sacrifice for the Son of God? Our salvation is from hell and perdition and we talk about making sacrifices?' What does that mean? It means that when we realise what we, as God's people, have been saved from (along with the reason for that salvation), we get a true perspective on our sacrifice. Calling our actions sacrifice is both wrong and rude: would you hand your fiancée flowers with a note that says 'I give you these as a sign of my great sacrifice' or hand them over with a mumbled 'I got you these to shut you up'? Of course you wouldn't. So why, then, do we insist on labelling our Christian acts as sacrifice? According to Mr Chambers, these very acts should be the overflow of our love for him, and should be found throughout our lives.

There is a lot of talk these days about being radical. But being radical isn't about worshipping to drum 'n' bass and banging prayer sticks. It's about obedience. How can we get it right during the Sunday service if we can't sort it out during the week? How can there ever be radical worship in church, if day by day, out there, I'm not being obedient? If I'm not seeking to deny myself, take up my cross and follow him? We must learn to leave behind our own interests and agendas, and choose to serve others first. Then we will be his disciples. If making and believing that statement does not affect how we are at work, college or school, then, unfortunately it is just words.

The danger here is that this book gets promptly put down to collect dust. 'Oh Mike,' you may think, 'stick to those funny little stories you tell.' The trouble is that this issue won't go away. If we don't learn to obey God's commands, then we will struggle to get past first base. It doesn't all have to be doom and gloom though, for as Jesus pointed out, 'he who seeks to gain his life will lose it. He who loses his life for my sake and for the gospel will find it.' Believe me, when Jesus talks about finding life, he means it, in all the technicolour glory that was first intended.

Joyful sacrifice is a theme that runs deep throughout the whole Bible, surfacing with particular momentum in Luke 19: 'Jesus entered Jericho and was passing through. A man was there by the name of Zacchaeus. He was a chief tax collector and was wealthy' (vv. 1–2). What does that mean? It certainly does not mean that he worked for the government, that he was a respectable, upright civil servant. He worked for the occupying power, the enemy. His activities cursed Israel and embarrassed his community. He was regarded as a traitor, and not just a low grade one at that. No, Zacchaeus was high up in the traitor business, rising through the ranks to reach the pole position of chief tax collector. As such, his job description was fairly simple: take money from his own people, give some to the Romans, take a few bribes and backhanders and pocket whatever else he fancied. As an outcast he wasn't doing too badly either, probably having reached the level of being gobbed on in the street and generally ignored. His social circle would have consisted of whatever other social outcasts were around. He was certainly wealthy, probably lonely and quite possibly unhappy.

'He wanted to see who Jesus was, but being a short man he could not, because of the crowd. So he ran ahead and climbed a sycamore fig-tree to see him, since Jesus was coming that way' (vv. 3–4). Zacchaeus had heard about Jesus and he wanted to see who he was. So, he climbed up a sycamore tree which was a pretty strange thing for a tax collector to do; it neither enhanced his credibility nor protected his person. But he was desperate, and the tree was his only chance.

'When Jesus reached the spot, he looked up and said to him, "Zacchaeus, come down immediately" ' (v. 5). Now I don't know exactly what happened there, but I just wonder whether when Jesus said that to him, Zacchaeus thought, 'Oh no, he's going to have a go at me; he's seen me and he knows who I am.' And the crowd around who would have known him might have been saying, 'Go on, if you're the Messiah, slay him.'

But then Jesus would have stunned them all by saying, 'Tonight, I am coming to your house for dinner.' It's brilliant. Only Jesus would say something like that. There were the religious leaders, there were the Pharisees, there were the respectable people and Jesus looks up at the tree and he says, 'I've seen you, Zacchaeus, and I know your name. I know your name so come down, I'm inviting myself around for dinner.' In the Scriptures eating together is seen as an intimate act (which is why, in the Song of Songs, it says, 'He brought me to his banqueting table and his banner over me is love'). Jesus wasn't announcing his intention to check out Zacchaeus' line in hors d'oeuvres and internal décor, he was telling him that he wanted to share fellowship with him.

> All the people saw this and began to mutter, 'He has gone to be the guest of a "sinner".'
> But Zacchaeus stood up and said to the Lord, 'Look, Lord! Here and now I give half of my possessions to the poor, and if I have cheated anybody out of anything, I will pay back four times the amount.'
> Jesus said to him, 'Today, salvation has come to this house because this man, too, is a son of Abraham. For the Son of Man came to seek and to save what was lost.' (vv. 7–10)

You see, the fruit of what Jesus was saying was that Zacchaeus welcomed him gladly and took him home. If we really know what we've been saved from as Zacchaeus did, then we welcome Jesus in, and are ready to change. Because that simple act of asking to go to his house was in such stark contrast to the usual treatment that he received from others, Zacchaeus understood his salvation, and responded with amazing, generous, overflowing, abandoned obedience. Giving away half of his possessions as well as four times the amount he had swindled was no mean feat. Neither was Jesus's response: 'Today, salvation has come to this house.' Salvation didn't come when Zacchaeus declared his intention to relieve himself of so much of his wealth; it actually came much earlier on when Jesus told him to get down from the tree and put the kettle on. It is not our sacrifice that saves us; rather that sacrifice should be an automatic, joyful response to understanding how much we've been forgiven. Zacchaeus' generosity was the fruit of his salvation. Our sacrifice of obedience isn't out of duty but it's out of a massive overflow of our love for Jesus. God's calling us to be radical Christians. We too have received his salvation: now it's time to respond.

In the early days of the Jesus Movement, an American evangelistic phenomenon which started in California in the 1960s and 70s, young people everywhere were having their first encounters with Jesus Christ. The Christians had started doing crazy things to spread the gospel like opening up coffee bars on the beaches (perhaps that doesn't sound so crazy after all, but you get my drift). This might be an off the wall thought, but if God is intending us to impact a generation, then the chances are that, as with all other areas of culture, the tolerance levels have risen. Think about films, music and literature; censorship levels have dramatically slacked off over the years. Attitudes to family, race and nationality have also changed, becoming less structured and rigid. Surely, then, the methods that we need to employ to reach people will need to be crazier than those of thirty years ago. I'm not suggesting that we set up our coffee bars actually in the sea, but we might like to keep in mind the fact that it is good to be in a place where we feel the adrenaline rush. Where we may not know if something will work, where the consequences of failure could be personally embarrassing, but the desire is to do it for God. Worship is to do these things. To sing the songs and not live the life is not worship.

Dietrich Bonhoeffer, a German Christian who was executed during the Second World War because of his involvement in resistance to Hitler, said, 'When Christ calls a man, he bids him come and die.' Wesley says in one of his hymns, 'Let earth no more my heart divide, with Christ may I be crucified.'

Both of these are vital truths. God calls us to this, not that he may squeeze more out of us, but because he wants to put more into us. This is the secret of a joy-filled life: to no longer be your own but to be his. Jesus's own life was a perfect model of this: obedience was his food, the thing that gave him life. He obeyed his Father, and told us that if we love him, we will obey his commands. It's as simple as that.

3

The Language of Worship

We worship in many different ways – through creativity and dedication, expression and commitment, song and work. It's like a love affair. If I asked you how you knew you were loved, chances are that you would come up with evidence ranging from gifts and words to sacrifices and actions. There is also another way that we know that we are loved, it is by the way that we feel. This state is indescribable and it belongs to the bizarre realm of the heart. Traditional, logical explanations fail to work here. For example, how ridiculous does it sound to describe a kiss as the mutual oral exchange of molecules and saliva? No, here description is difficult.

In the same way that there are different kinds of love, there are different kinds of worship: the worship that comes from our lips, the worship that comes from our lives, and the worship that comes from our hearts. Within each area are codes and formats, methods of expression and limitations of use. Together, they make up the language of worship.

The Language of our Hearts

A.W. Tozer said that 'true worship is to be so person-ally and hopelessly in love with God, that the idea of a transfer of affection never even remotely exists.'

I've used this quote so often that I'm in danger of wearing it out, but it remains a fantastic turn of phrase. Could you envisage being so besotted as to be blind to even the most attractive alternative? At times it feels as if reaching that state is pure fantasy, but there are occasions when God pulls a few surprises out of the bag. This always reminds me of a youth group I met once.

It was at a particularly Christian Christian event, where certain delegates were not too happy with their lot – you know the sort: disaffected young people, dragged along by their parents who hope that they will meet some nice young Christians and get back on the right track. Their kids, however, reluctantly see it as a fine opportunity to meet some young innocents, in-dulge in a little soul corruption and get high in a tent for a few days. So, at this particular event where I was working, there were plenty of these people on the fringe. Occasionally they would pop into one of the main meetings to see what was going on, but generally they stuck to their tents where their supply of cheap narcotics was keeping them happy.

Something must have gone badly wrong, as on the penultimate day we had a full complement of them in the meeting. It made me happy, as well as slightly nervous – these were the sort of people I used to be scared of when I was their age – but I managed to convince myself that as long as I didn't establish eye contact my lunch money and satchel would remain intact.

The meeting progressed. As we drew to a close, we did a U-turn and went into a spontaneous time of worship, something that just seemed like the right thing to do. I began to worry that my fringe friends had thought it the wrong thing to do, when after a while I spied them marching up towards me from the back of the hall. They had the exits covered and there was no escape. I closed my eyes and hoped for the best.

A few days later it all made sense. I had been confused when they had handed over their various 'naughties' (condoms, knives, spliffs and such like), and slightly embarrassed when I had been spotted packing the evidence away in the boot of my car. Why had they decided to give it all away? It was because of Tozer. That quote about a 'transfer of affections' described them exactly. During the worship they had met with God – I had seen it myself – and it affected them. Once they had touched the eternal, they no longer had the desire to waste their affections on the little things. Worship can be like that: it can be the language of the heart – an unheard, untranslatable tongue that communicates directly and profoundly. I have been a youth worker for so long that I am probably reaching my sell-by date. One of the hardest things I have to do as a youth worker is the sex talk. It is not that I am particularly embarrassed by the subject. It is more that it comes up with such monotonous regularity. I could give the sex talk in my sleep. The point is that I wonder if it makes a lot of difference. I have noticed, however, that when people really meet Jesus and have that intimate exchange with him in worship then they want to do what pleases him. There has been a transfer of affections. The word the Bible uses to describe this is repentance. This literally means 'to turn around' or to change your mind and your actions. Repentance is also worship, it is responding to Jesus by choosing to live a life of obedience to him.

Tozer also went on to examine the issue of idolatry: that we are created to worship, and we will worship either God or other gods. 'Idolatry', he claimed, 'is to entertain thoughts about God which are unworthy of him.' Now this one had me confused. What, I first thought, has thinking got to do with idolatry? The lights came on when I realised that thinking unworthy thoughts about God makes thought an idol; it downgrades God's worth and means that we construct something that is not truly God – we get God-lite, an easy to swallow yet less than nutritious brand. Our task is not simply to turn from false idols, but to understand that turning from idols means banishing misconceptions about who God is.

The Language of our Hands

Question: Is it possible to express passionate, intimate devotion and adoration without the use of our bodies? Answer: Yes, but you have to be in a coma. Later we will examine the Hebrew words for worship, as well as those used in the New Testament. Many of those used in the Hebrew to describe acts of worship are very interesting; nearly all of them signify a specific physical posture. To bless in the Hebrew literally means to kneel before. In the Psalms, so many of the commands are to do physical things. We are all familiar with phrases like 'I lift my eyes up to the mountains', 'lift up your heads to the coming King', 'I will lift up my hands . . .'. These are the physical expressions of joy, praise and thanksgiving. Alongside these are those that express our humility and God's sovereignty, the kneeling down of verses such as, 'Come, let us bow down in worship, let us kneel before the Lord our Maker' (Psalm 95:6). On a slightly more trying level are the physical expressions of tearing clothes and wearing sackcloth and ashes when in mourning.

It seems pretty clear from the Bible that the Hebrews were a very physical group of people. I don't mean that they were into spontaneous bouts of all-in wrestling or that they greeted each other with vice-like headlocks. But we know, from their worship, that they weren't shy about using their bodies (remember that whole loincloth thing that David had going?). Still, drawing on cultural reference points from the past can often be a red herring when it comes to the present. Relevance seems to fade severely over the years, and of course, no church would want to make people do things they were uncomfortable with. I can explain this better by giving you an example. I struggle with the whole dancing issue. Not having been blessed with a thoroughly accurate sense of rhythm, I tend to look rather like a drunken Elvis impersonator on the rare occasions that I get up and 'strut' my stuff. At times my inner monologue contains a battle between the belief that dance was a pivotal act in Old Testament worship, and the knowledge that my moves would have people doubled over in hysterics, thinking about Hound Dog and muscular spasms.

Obviously it's stupid to be using worship as an excuse for putting on a show to impress the locals. However, there is a case for the argument that spending a worship time sitting down with arms folded, looking glum, is perhaps not the best indication of a heart that is on fire for God. We know from lessons in communications that we express far more through our actions than our words. It has been said that the eyes are the window to the soul. As an extension to this I would like to suggest that the buttocks are the Venetian blinds of the spirit: sat down, drawn and immovable we keep the light out.

In the Hebrew culture there was a great understanding of who we are as human beings. Instead of subscribing to the belief that we are spirits trapped inside our bodies, there was a common belief that spirit and flesh were mirror images of each other. The inference of this is that our bodies are meant to reflect what is in our hearts, especially when we are worshipping our Maker. Like a fake smile, outward manifestations can be used to try and convince others, but that is nothing more than hypocrisy. At the same time, if the love of God is in your heart, you're meant to (in fact, you're almost commanded to) express that through your body. Sometimes we say that, for example, dancing or raising our hands in worship is not part of our culture, that we're 'not that type'. These barriers are man-made; we were all made to laugh, dance, sing and do all manner of things to express joy. In explaining this we come across a central point to understanding the language of worship: this language

32

is not simply saying the words, 'I bless you, Lord, I give you thanks', it is a matter of using the whole body to express those things as well. Many times in Scriptures we see that hands and hearts are mentioned in the same breath, particularly in the context of worship. Psalm 24 is just one example: 'Who may stand in his holy place? He who has clean hands and a pure heart.' It was assumed that if God touched your heart then that would be expressed through your body in worship and also in acts of obedience. There is a saying: 'When God has our hearts our hands will follow.'

Such a style of expression has of late been finding its way back into the Church. But we have only just begun to do this, and there is a long way to go before we can declare that we have fully captured the spirit of David as he danced, fully abandoned and 90 per cent naked before his God. His wife may have been offended at his behaviour, but her problems should not become our defences. She was Saul's daughter, and the dancing incident was one of many in which she looked down on David. Bitterly she said to him, 'How the king of Israel has distinguished himself today, disrobing in the sight of the slave girls as any vulgar fellow would' (2 Samuel 6:20). David's reply was 'you ain't seen nothing yet', as he ranted on about becoming even more undignified. He was worshipping in his underpants, and he threatened to go further. Whatever it took for him to be able to express his devotion was on the menu. He was allowing himself to be abandoned in his praise and thanksgiving. Sometimes that's a decision we all have to make: to do whatever is necessary to express our feelings for God.

I remember Martin Smith from Delirious? telling

33

me how bad he was at dancing. Quite why he chose to tell me I'm not sure – he must have felt safe having viewed my Elvis impersonations – but if we're really honest, he still is pretty terrible. Well, he decided at one stage that he was fed up of not dancing, and that he was going to have a go. He began in his church, having felt that he didn't want to be hindered any longer. So he started, choosing to run around the church hall. He ran around for a bit, and then thought 'I don't care what anyone thinks,' and then he started to jump. Now, you've probably seen him, jumping when he's on stage. For Martin, overcoming his psychological barriers in order to worship further was a conscious decision. In our churches we need to encourage others to do this without nagging them. That doesn't mean we condemn as sinners those who don't do the same as us, but it does mean explaining that sometimes worship is an act of the will. Sometimes it does mean taking the decision to worship with my body as well as with my mind, as well as with my lips.

The Language of the Bible

Many of us feel that we were blessed with a natural aversion to all things tricky. My personal list has taken in a variety of pet-hates over the years – from wallpaper stripping to getting my car taxed on time each year – but there's one that unites many of us: study. An obvious point, I know, but getting down to a solid hour's worth of biblical exegesis often comes a distant second to watching televised repeats of the 1986 West Sussex indoor bowls championships. I doubt that I can single-handedly change all that, but I do believe that taking a magnifying glass to the biblical presentation of worship can yield some rather dramatic results. Unlike bowls.

So here goes, a little study of some of the biblical words used to describe acts of worship in the Bible.

Shacah – This is the most common word for worship in the Old Testament and means to bow down. Bowing is an attitude of submission and obedience.

Hallel – Used ninety-nine times in the Old Testament, *hallel* means to praise, to boast of, to celebrate and (I love this bit) to be clamorously foolish. Doesn't that say it all? It is the root word of hallelujah.

Yadar – Meaning thanksgiving. It literally means 'to extend the hand'. This 'extension of the hand' gets used ninety times throughout the Old Testament; fifty-three times in praise, thirty-two times as to give thanks, sixteen times as to confess and five times as thanks.

Tehillah and *zamar* are both words that appear in the original Hebrew, and refer to singing. *Tehillah* means to sing to the Lord as part of the singing of hallelujah. *Zamar* is singing when accompanied by musical instruments. When the Puritans did away with all music in order for their worship to be 100 per cent God focused, despite their best intentions, they were actually being unscriptural. In the Hebrew culture worship is not divorced from life, instead we worship with the gifts of life.

Samach – To be glad, to rejoice. This word implies an outburst of spontaneous joy which overflows into some physical action.

Moving into the New Testament, *proskuneo* (a personal favourite of mine) – This means to come to-wards to kiss, and was used to describe worship. It gets sixty-six hits throughout the New Testament, and has the added advantage of being able to describe the act of a hound licking his master's hand.

Then we find the words *eucharisto* and *eucharistia,* which are Greek for 'thank you'. From this we get the word 'Eucharist' which is another name for the communion service and sets communion in the context of thanksgiving. Communion is a wonderful way to worship God. As we take the bread and the wine we remember the death of Jesus on the cross and we also celebrate that we are a forgiven people who have been reconciled to our Father. Communion re-pre-sents the sacrifice of the Lamb of God and draws from us a sacrifice of praise. In the words of C.T. Studd, 'If Jesus be the Son of God and he died for me, then no sacrifice that I make for him can be too great.'

The heart of worship is intimacy. All worship roads should lead there and it is in the place of intimacy that we receive power to live a life of sacrificial, devoted worship in the world. There's a chance that all this could seem slightly irrelevant to some. To many, the act of intimate adoration of our Father comes second to 'doing things for him'. While I in no way wish to deny the importance of practical deeds, I'm reminded of the story in John 12 of Jesus's meeting with the sinful woman, Mary Magdalene. She poured a jar of very expensive perfume (it was worth a year's wages) over Jesus. Her abandonment riled Judas to the point that he complained that the perfume could have been put to better use. There were plenty of other worthy causes that could have used the cash. And today, there are always evangelistic missions to be funded, churches to be extended and projects to realise. At the same time, there is also Jesus. Constant and true, he looks for the same behaviour from us that he found in Mary: waste. He wants us to waste everything we have on him: our money, our talents, our time and our energy. The place of offering is there at his feet, and is always open to our approach.

It's unusual to think of worship as being expensive. While we may nod and offer the occasional 'hear hear' as we think of approaching God with sincere and intimate hearts, it seems to me that worship sessions often have fairly short shopping lists. When, for example, did your church last discuss the purchase of white robes, golden crowns or a rainbow that looks like an emerald? This brings us to the thorny issue of the adorning of churches. When so many of the world's population live in poverty, a solid gold lectern can seem like a tasteless way to spend some cash. Yet does that mean that the colouring of our worship is forever condemned to the muted tones of the worship leader's latest jumper from Mr Byright? Thankfully, the answer is a resounding no. This issue is another chapter, another book maybe, but as a small offering I would suggest that true worship is inseparable from justice (and that really is another chapter). I mean that when God has our hearts, we get his too.

And so we return to the point of sacrifice. The worship saucepan contains many ingredients, and two of them are creativity and sacrifice. The language of worship is sacrifice. Sometimes it might mean doing things that we're not terribly comfortable with. That is good for us. Obviously we have to be careful to avoid imposing our behavioural expectations on others, but we cannot deny that at times, the Lord plainly asks us how much we love him. Are we prepared to sacrifice ourselves for him?

4

The Fruit of Worship –
Part 1 Healing

We worship because he deserves it, because worship is the expression of intimacy with him. Whenever we worship him there is a consequence; at times that means we get changed or healed, but it can also mean that our levels of holiness increase. These next two chapters look at both of those fruits.

The title I've chosen for this book hints at the idea that worship is not supposed to be for us, but for him. It is not a question of our gaining anything from it, in fact it hardly matters if we find a particular session exciting or fun. Worship is God's, not ours. However, despite the ridiculous nature of a comment like 'I really got a lot out of the worship today', there seems to be some kind of loophole: you see, when we worship, we always get something back. God cannot be out-given in generosity – 'give and it will be given to you, pressed down, shaken together, running over, it will be poured into your lap' said Jesus. As we give, we always get something back and particularly in worship. However, it's not worship if we decide that we will worship in order to get something back: that's an exchange. God's into giving, not exchanging.

Of course, the first question that any self-respecting Christian shouldn't ask is, 'What's in it for me?' However, that doesn't usually stop me from drawing up a quick, guilt-laden list of the personal pros and cons attached to any new activity I may undertake. Except when it comes to worship: worship I can see as his.

I wasn't always this wise, though. It was only after a particularly bumpy start to my Christian life that things began to level out and I got some sense into my head. It was about the time of my A levels, and my mind had become obsessed with the concept of rewards. For months, the Mike Pilavachi Universe acted like a cheap garage promotion. If I revised for an hour, I would allow myself to phone up some friends. If I read a study guide, I was granted a trip to the cinema. Soon I began saving up my rewards, in the hope of justifying a week of reckless partying right in the middle of my exams. I was a mess, and it is little wonder to me now that my spiritual world-view became warped at the same time. God, I thought, deserved our worship, but in that day and age, one-way giving seemed so stale, so passé. I decided that the whole worship thing needed pepping up. 'If I worship you every day for a month' went my proposal to the Lord, 'then you can give me a car.'

I never did find out whether God had accepted my deal; I lost interest after the first week of daily devotions. At the time I thought it was a lucky escape for the Almighty, but since then I've come round to the idea that it was me who got off lightly. It has since been pointed out to me that worship is not a transaction, nor is it an open invitation for blackmail.

Change

Another endearing character trait that I adopted early on in my Christian life was the belief that change would come rapidly. Part of this stemmed from the fact that my Greek heritage had endowed me with the ability to grow what for most teenage boys would amount to a week's facial hair growth in just under an afternoon. Gifts of the Spirit, I logically concluded, were bound to be like beards: quick to arrive and reasonably easy to maintain. I needed a fair amount of sorting out when I first met God, and I had it in mind to get it all done by Christmas, leaving me ready to take on the conversion of Harrow by Easter. It didn't happen.

You know what they say about watched kettles? It's the same deal with change: it seems as if it takes an eternity when you watch it like a hawk. Change takes time, and I've discovered that it is a gradual process, not something that happens overnight – although that is possible. I've also noticed that when I look at myself intently, picking over every move, mood and reaction I usually see no sign of change at all. When I reach the end of the week and wonder how much more loving, tender, compassionate and generally brilliant I am, I usually return with a decisive zero. But things do start to happen when I forget about myself and look at God. Somehow the Holy Spirit sneaks up and changes me. While it seems to take a very long time, and while there is an awful long way still to go, something has happened.

Healing and Wholeness

Doctors are labelling many of the problems that we experience today – our sicknesses and illnesses – as being psychosomatic. The physical symptoms can have psychological roots, and (based on the belief that as many as 60 per cent of illnesses are stress related) many surgeries are now employing professional counsellors to help patients deal with stress. When the Bible talks about the 'root of bitterness', we talk about a bad self-image. This could be a contributing factor in any number of conditions, from asthma to arthritis, cancer to colitis. It is interesting that lately, as a Church, we in the UK have seen far more emotional healings than we have seen physical. Some people have seen this as a reason for sadness, explaining that living in 'miracle days' where the dead rise and the blind see on a daily basis is a sure sign that revival is close at hand. We do long to see more physical healing, signs and wonders and miracles. I personally long for that. However let us give thanks for what God is doing in binding up the broken-hearted. Often God is healing the cause rather than the symptom.

Let's put this hair-splitting of mine aside for a while: God is a God who heals. Over the last few years, many Christians have rediscovered the healing ministry, realising that it is permissible to ask (and expect) God to heal. When Jesus walked the earth two thousand years ago, he told the disciples that they would do the same things as he (and even greater) when he had gone to heaven. In the Acts of the Apostles, we see them casting out demons, healing people from various diseases and setting them free in the name of

Jesus. We see that praying for healing is one of the main indications that we are following Jesus. Clearly, we see much of this occurring via the 'hands on' technique, where the prayers are accompanied by a symbolic expression of faith (that God can heal) and desire (that God will heal). In our desire to follow Jesus in this way, we also must not ignore the healing that occurs as we worship. It may take a long time, but when we adore him we are set free.

My friend and colleague Matt Redman was part of the youth group that I inherited when I started to work at St Andrew's, Chorleywood. He was thirteen, and soon after he joined he told me that when he was seven years old his father committed suicide. His father sent Matt and his brother and sisters a note that said they would be better off without him. Then, two years later, his mother remarried and, after a period where things were good, they eventually went horribly wrong. Matt blamed himself for his father's death, and was afraid that if he said how unhappy he was, he would be the cause of another family break-up.

Eventually the pressure got so great that Matt told me how bad he was feeling. In the years that followed, I saw Matt's pain, his struggles and insecurities. I saw God heal Matt in an incredible way. It took many years, and it was as he worshipped that God healed him. If Matt's got an anointing for worship leading now, I'm sure it's because he genuinely found God in worship.

Many of the songs that he writes now come from that same place, and that is why they speak to people. 'I will offer up my life' starts one song,

in spirit and truth,
pouring out the oil of love
as my worship to you.
In surrender I must give
my every part
Lord, receive the sacrifice of a broken heart.

A broken heart was not written there to rhyme with 'every part': it was written because that's exactly where Matt comes from. We all need to learn to give the sacrifice when we are in pain.

While the process of healing for Matt was a long one, I suspect that at times God sped things up. There was one particular meeting we were taking part in, in those far-off days when the phrase Toronto blessing sounded more like a massage than a spiritual phenomenon. Anyway, we were supposed to be leading this thing, when suddenly Matt starts laughing, falling over and generally being drunk in the Holy Spirit. Eventually he had to be carried from the building back to his tent. Something happened at that meeting; he met with his Maker, Healer, Deliverer. In the months that followed the first signs of Matt's gift for songwriting began to emerge. God had given him something.

To worship is to find healing. Some of us have had to live with all sorts of things that have thrown us off course. As we devote ourselves to worship we get drawn up like a plant towards the sun, the heat and the light of God's love healing us, leaving us upright instead of bent double.

A New Perspective

To worship is also to gain a new perspective on life. Sometimes we can almost cherish our negative attitudes towards life and the world. When I was younger, I had experienced what seemed like more than my fair share of disappointments. Things that were promised never seemed to materialise, and I got into the habit of believing that good things would never happen to me. Imagining the worst case scenario, I thought, was a sure-fire way of avoiding disappointment. What I discovered later in life, was that believing the worst also left me a miserable git.

It has taken time for that to change. As we gaze at heaven and then take our eyes and place them on the world, heaven affects our vision – Son blindness, if you like. It affects the way we see our life. I believe that God has a plan for my life, that he knows, loves and will look after me. It may not be pain free, but, ultimately, God is in charge and I'm going to see him face to face. Even in the pain, there will be good things that will bring a bit of light in. God is not a capricious God. Whatever your situation, however you see the world, as you worship you will be set free.

How?

It works like this. As we look at God, getting a vision of heaven, we get his perspective on the world. 'You', said Jesus, 'shall know the truth and the truth shall set you free.' One of the things Jesus was alluding to there was that in knowing the truth, we get to know him – after all, he is the way, the truth and the life – but also, we begin to absorb more of God's understanding: the truth. The falsehoods in our lives then get exposed, and through worship of a loving, majestic God, we realise that his loving kindness does endure forever. We gradually begin to believe it, and we move from earthbound untruths to heavenly inspired absolutes.

When we work out that the God we worship is the Creator and boss of the entire universe, even when things don't go so well for us, then problems and disappointments no longer seem quite so bad. After all, as the ultimate boss, who are we to argue when he seems to take things in a slightly different direction to the one we had in mind?

For example, when bad things happened to Joseph – being sold into slavery etc. – he decided not to get bitter. He told his brothers years later that what they meant for harm God meant for good. 'God sent me ahead of you to save your lives by a great deliverance,' he said (see Genesis 45). If Joseph had refused to forgive his brothers, then all his claims about God's greatness, all his worship and devotion, would have meant nothing. If we are to have integrity, if our worship is to have integrity, then it must spill over to the attitudes of our lives.

We Christians have often been on the receiving end of the criticism that we can be too heavenly minded to be any earthly use. I think the same can be said the other way around: that we can also be too earthly minded to be any heavenly use. When we are heavenly minded in the best way, then we are fit for a life on earth. It helps when we see things the right way around, get things in the right order, when we realise our place in the universe.

5

The Fruit of Worship –
Part 2 Holiness

I used to be more of a man than I am today. In fact, at one point, there was about one-third more to Mike Pilavachi, most of it acting as the human equivalent of an airbag. In short, I was cuddly (so long as you had very long arms). In the fat-free year that was my 1998, I grilled, steamed and panted my way through mountains of fish, vegetables and virtual miles on my treadmill. I became so obsessed with the fat content of all food that my prayer life began to take on a distinctly dietary flavour. 'Oh Lord,' I would pipe up in church, 'restrict our intake of harmful sin, and raise our metabolic rate so that we too may deliver new converts faster than a bowl of pure fibre.' People soon got the message.

While I was changing on the outside, I was also hoping that I might get a 'two for one' deal on the inside – as if, by way of reward for all my hard work, God might give my soul a little tweak and make me into a more holy Christian. Unfortunately that wasn't to be, and at the end of the year I had to content myself with a very large collection of very, very large trousers.

What I did discover was that while hard work and discipline can do wonders for the gut, they do very little for the soul. I was hoping that I could work my way into God's good books, that a little spiritual sweat would deliver the goods. Eventually I saw the light, and realised that sanctification (the technical word for being made holy), like salvation, has nothing to do with our hard work, and everything to do with God's mighty grace. We can see this revelation plastered all throughout the Gospels – ask yourself who, from prostitutes to tax collectors, actually deserved Jesus's time, let alone his healing? – and for each of us, it should be the cause of a sigh of relief. Sanctification is a gift from God. In the same way that Jesus bought our forgiveness by offering himself as a sacrifice on the cross, so too he lets us hitch a ride and approach God, as he becomes our holiness.

True holiness is so much more than self-discipline. Repeating a list of 'Must Nots' (I must not be jealous, I must not be angry, I must not get bitter . . ., etc.) is not the way to bring about the desired results (unless, of course, the desired result is that you lose both your sanity and your friends). Even at our best, we could never match up to Christ's standards of holiness. It therefore makes sense to be on our knees asking Jesus to make us more holy by his power, not by ours.

With a little detective work it soon becomes clear that the Bible contains much on this subject. In fact, in Colossians, Paul tempts us with the declaration that he is about to reveal the secret that has been hidden through the ages. Apparently this particular secret was to be kept hidden from people until Christ had died and risen. Paul is the one charged with the task of revealing the mystery, and he drops the bomb in chapter 1 verse 27. Here goes: 'Christ in you, the hope of glory'.

Excuse me? Is that it – the secret that was hidden for so long? 'Christ in you, the hope of glory.' It doesn't make sense, does it? Even my computer struggles to understand it and underlines it in green, unable to suggest any reasonable alternative. Then it hit me. Take out the word 'you' and replace it with your name, and swap the word 'hope' for 'prospect'. Imagine it's an election campaign slogan and it starts to make sense: Christ in Mike, the prospect of glory. With Jesus in my life, there is a chance of things being better, of me being more holy, of final glory.

Things become even clearer when you check some more of Paul's letters. Turn to Galatians 2:20 and read as he expands this idea of our powerlessness to change ourselves and our reliance on heavenly assistance: 'I have been crucified with Christ,' he writes, 'it is no longer I who live but Christ who lives in me.' That's exactly what it means to have Christ living in us, by his Spirit. In the same way that God's incarnation involved him becoming human flesh, so too has Jesus become incarnated in his Church, his body. As Christians and members of that body, we have the chance to be intimately involved with him through the Church and through our relationship with him. We are meant to be a people of his presence; we are supposed to interact with our Maker, to have him at the centre of our lives. This, as I'm sure you can imagine, is good news for anyone wanting to be more holy.

The Place of Worship

Before this sends hoards of people off thinking that God hands out holiness to all and sundry like a senile Santa at Christmas, perhaps I ought to set the record straight. Remember that this is in the context of worship – it comes when we have relationship with God.

Worship is central to this whole process. If we are really going to get to grips with our ambition to become more holy, more like our Saviour, then we simply must devote ourselves to worship. It's a well-known fact that people become influenced by their surroundings, a theory that is supported by all manner of examples, from the type of music played to super-market shoppers to the behaviour of British tourists on the Costa del Sol.

I pick up accents faster than I used to pick up a cream cake, and, in particular, whenever I visit South Africa, I return having adopted a nasal quality to my voice and a batch of stock phrases such as 'Ya, ya' and 'See you just now'. When people finally understand what I'm saying, they often think I'm mimicking them on purpose, but the truth is that I cannot help it. So join the dots here: if when you hang out with people you start thinking or sounding a bit like them, how much more will time spent with the Lord our God produce desirable side effects? How do we hang out with the Lord? Primarily, through worship, through intimate relationship.

This idea that being with him is to become like him is backed up by Paul's second letter to the Cor-inthians, where he writes: 'Now the Lord is the Spirit, and where the Spirit of the Lord is, there is freedom. And we, who with unveiled faces all reflect the Lord's glory, are being transformed into his likeness with ever-increasing glory which comes from the Lord who is the Spirit' (3:17–18). This pivotal verse about holiness deserves some unpacking. Paul had just been writing about Moses, pointing out how, after he had been up the mountain and seen God face-to-face, he had to cover his face with a veil as it shone so much. Paul tells of how, after that, the radiance that was covered by the veil began to fade away. You can imagine that, for Moses, simply being in God's presence was enough for him to come away from the meeting with something of God stuck on him. How much more, then, should we expect to be transformed by the time we spend with the Lord? Through the death of Jesus, a new covenant has been established between the two of us, one which encourages us to spend as much time as we can with him.

The key to this idea can be found in the word that has been translated as 'reflect', which the text tells us can also be taken to mean 'contemplate'. The translators obviously had a little bit of a ruck over this one, and the 'reflect' team won. It's good to see that those 'contemplate' boys didn't go down without a fight though, as their little addition opens the whole text up. The reason for their dilemma was that the actual Greek phrase that they were translating supported both interpretations. While 'reflect' and 'contemplate' seem to be on different sides of the camp when it comes to meaning, the translators discovered that the Greek original was linked to the act of looking into a mirror. When looking in a mirror, we both reflect and contemplate what we see before us: we perform the passive act of looking, as well being involved in the physical act of providing the mirror with an image to reflect. The original carries the idea that as we look at the Lord we will both understand more of him, and take on more of his qualities.

This is the same principle as when you hang out with someone a lot you start taking on his or her characteristics, especially if it is someone you love. It is a constant source of amazement how many adopted kids I meet that in many ways resemble adoptive parents, although, genetically, they are nothing like them. Somehow by being with them there is something that sparks an internal change which can be visible on the surface. The rule is exactly the same with Jesus: the more we look at him, the more we look like him, the more his character rubs off on ours.

This is an incredibly potent encouragement for us as Christians. If we want to become more like Jesus, the solution is neither navel gazing nor constipation; it won't come by sitting around waiting for God to get around to us when he has time, and nor will it come by us trying to force out the fruit of the Spirit. The good news is that being a Christian is not about attempting to pay God back by trying to be like him, it's about letting him be God in our lives. That means giving him time, space and respect. I have to let his character grow in me, and I can do that by hanging out with him. I have to look at him to reflect him, and just being with him can be enough. That's how worship is central to the Christian life: without it, we have no relationship with our God, and there is little chance of our being transformed into his likeness. If I want to become more holy, let me spend a few hours worshipping and I walk away with something of the shine on my face that Moses experienced. I haven't got to the stage of needing a veil yet, but I'm sure I've changed inside.

The fruit of the Spirit as described in Galatians 5 is set up as the main aim for us Christians. The collection of qualities combine to form a perfect description of Jesus himself, which sets the standard pretty high. Bearing in mind Paul's words about being 'transformed' through worship, it seems that these character improvements aren't as hard to develop as we may have first thought. Someone said once that we shouldn't pray, 'Lord give me joy/love/patience,' but that we should say, 'Lord, I want more of you in me.' As in all the best supermarket promotions bulk buying can bring the highest rewards, it's the same with Jesus. Why bust a gut trying desperately to improve levels of self-control when you can get the whole package by being 'transformed into his likeness'?

The concept of Christ living within us can seem kind of strange, almost unnatural. Paul used the same phrases to illustrate an intimacy and a radical commitment to his Creator. Let us return to Galatians 2:20 where Paul says, 'I have been crucified with Christ and I no longer live, but Christ lives in me.' The more we look at him, the more his character and his personality begin to be lived out in us. In a way, the idea of having Christ living in us ties in with those sweets you find at the seaside – the sticks of rock that have a message that runs all the way through. We're meant to be like that rock with the words on the inside and not just on the outside. That is something that only Jesus can do and it is a fruit of worship, something which takes time.

We've mentioned the fruit of the Spirit, and it is important to note that it is the Spirit's fruit and not ours. Going a little further with this idea, we know that fruit trees aren't exactly flexible when it comes down to production; a pear tree won't give you apples any more than a banana tree will provide strawberries. No amount of concentration, hard work or fertiliser will help either tree divert from its genetic script. The fruit of the Spirit is a description of the character of Jesus, and the only person who can bear the fruit of the Spirit is Jesus.

What is more, you don't see many fruit trees getting all stressed when it comes round to delivering the goods; the process is as natural as they come. Only Jesus can tease out those characteristics from within us of love, joy, peace, patience, kindness, goodness, gentleness, humility and self-control. It comes naturally to him.

Another problem that I used to encounter in the whole 'fruit arena', was that I wanted my spiritual development to be instantaneous. 'Give me more patience,' I once demanded of the Lord, 'now.' Fruit growing always takes a full season. You cannot expect the apples to be hours away as soon as the blossom arrives; instead, you need to allow the development to take place over the months and years. Once the period of basking in the summer sun is over the apples tend to be ready, but only then.

I used to examine myself regularly for fruit growth. Were my anger levels subsiding? How was that baby shoot of patience I first noticed last week? Had the love cutting taken root yet? It was only when someone pointed out to me that the trees themselves don't tend to get much in the way of gratification when they produce fruit, that I realised where I had been going wrong. The fruits of the Spirit – the by-products of our worship – are not there to be measured by us, they're not even there for us. Instead, they are there for the benefit of those around us.

This whole fruit imagery is pretty basic stuff, but in a way I think that we need to be reminded of just how fundamental the truth of all this is: if we spend time with God, we grow closer to him.

Straight after Paul's bit about unveiled faces, we are offered some further thoughts on holiness.

> But we have this treasure in jars of clay to
> show that this all-surpassing power is from God
> and not from us. We are hard pressed on every
> side, but not crushed; perplexed but not in
> despair; persecuted but not abandoned; struck
> down, but not destroyed. We always carry
> around in our body the death of Jesus, so that
> the life of Jesus may also be revealed in our
> body. (2 Corinthians 4:7–10)

Sometimes we have our brains set to the wrong frequency and we end up misinterpreting so many things. We get confused about the fruit of the Spirit, and we get it all wrong about victory, glory and holiness. The truth is that we will always be the jars of clay and God the treasure. There's some teaching doing the rounds in the Church which gives the impression that we are the treasure who only have to 'name it to claim it'.

Let me explain. Paul's analogy was particularly relevant to his audience at the time. In the first century there were no banks, and there were no safety deposit boxes. Anything of worth had to be looked after by the owner. The more prosperous folk, those who wanted to keep something of value for their old age or to pass on when they died, would look for suitable hiding places in their own homes. Obviously, one of the places that would have been way down on any list of top hiding places would have been a valuable vase. You can imagine the scenario: thief nicks the vase and unwittingly gets the fancy jewellery too. He's very happy, the owner's very sad. So what the rich people used to do in those days, and it actually became well known so I'm surprised that the thieves didn't suss it, was to get ordinary clay pots and use them as hiding places for their most valuable possessions.

Do you know, it's the same with us; we're jars of clay. We're not great ornamental vases. We're jars of clay, broken pots. Many of us are broken pots in whom God has chosen to put his treasure, the treasure of his life, the treasure of the life of his Son. He puts it in my jar of clay and that is the secret of the Christian faith: it is not being something I am not but it is Jesus being who he is through me. This is what radiates life. Straight after talking about treasure in jars of clay, Paul says, 'We are hard pressed on every side but not crushed; perplexed but not in despair.' It's wonderful because it's a twofold thing – I find him in my weakness.

According to Paul, God sees us this way too. We're unworthy, yet he still trusts us with his treasure. Paul explains how it works. We are hard pressed on every side but not crushed. We are 'perplexed but not in despair'. That feels like an accurate description of me throughout most of my life: perplexed but not quite in despair. I used to think that it was wrong to be perplexed, that true faith has no room for doubt. To find Paul saying 'perplexed but not in despair; persecuted but not abandoned; struck down but not destroyed' was a fantastic relief. We don't have to pretend to be something we're not, we can approach God in our weakness and pain. How does this apply to worship? Because we are meant to come to God in worship with all our pain and frustrations, without holding anything back.

There's that wonderful place in the Scriptures at the end of 2 Corinthians where Paul says, '. . . there was given me a thorn in my flesh, a messenger of Satan to torment me. Three times I pleaded with the Lord to take it from me. But he said to me, "My grace is sufficient for you, for my power is made perfect in weakness" ' (12:7–9). Whatever it was – perhaps a physical problem like his eyesight, or a relationship problem that couldn't get healed, some even say it was with his wife – the point is that there was something he struggled with. The point is that Paul was a jar of clay, and like us, there was no need for him to be ashamed of his weakness.

Until recently I couldn't tell you the story of what happened to me when I was young. I only told it for the first time a year and a half ago in Norway, but I am learning that my healing and wholeness is a progression, and that I don't need to expect immediate solutions. That is what the Lord wants to do for, in and through you.

57

6

Prophetic Intercession

This is my dream: I'm standing in a crowded bus station, with people on all sides straining to see the buses as they pull up in front of us. Everyone is either whistling or humming, causing the station to echo with an eerie sonic trifle. As the buses pull in, they let off all their passengers. None of them are whistling, or humming. Instead they all look exhausted. They fall to the floor and sleep. In time they get up – revived by their rest – and begin to join in the chorus with their own whistled or hummed tunes. No one ever gets on the bus, instead the crowd seem more intent on catching each driver's eye as they arrive. Often they too seem tired, but the noise and atmosphere in the depot spurs them on. They seem to get recharged quicker than their beleaguered passengers, and before long they drive their buses back out of the station. Now put this on the back burner until the end of the chapter.

There are times when we aren't totally honest with God in our worship. In charismatic circles, we have been guilty of being bogus worship junkies, desperate to lose ourselves in an hour of exuberant worship to wash away the cares of a busy week. Surely, half a dozen happy worship songs sung back to back as a pick-me-up isn't quite the way that worship of the almighty God is supposed to be? Surely our worship should not be a means of escape from the world? If the Psalms are anything to go by, worship is supposed to be an opportunity to express the depth of our hearts to God.

Psalm 42 starts (as do quite a number of David's other psalms) with a declaration that the enemies have him surrounded, that God has abandoned him, that his tears flow throughout the night. Yet, it ends up with 'and yet will I rejoice in the Lord'. It seems that in the Church we are very good at getting on with the rejoicing bits, but not so good at expressing the despair.

I was challenged on this when I visited Graham Cray in Cambridge. Graham is Principal of Ridley Hall, Cambridge, a theological college and vicar factory. Occasionally Matt Redman and I go up to visit and chat things through. One particular time I asked Graham where he thought our worship was going wrong. Thinking quietly to myself, 'Go ahead, have a go at Redman,' I sat back and waited for his answer. He was very gracious and he started off saying to Matt, 'Well, I love your songs, they are so Christ centred.' Then he said, 'As you ask, the thing that I've always been wondering is generally, where is the place for lament in our worship?' Lament? I was confused. He pointed to the Psalms, the songs of exile, the ones about sitting down and weeping by the rivers of Babylon. All we do, he suggested, is sing the happy bits, the 'I will praise you, rejoice in you at all times' bits.

I must admit to feeling sorry for the poor bloke. Too much theology had obviously affected his perception. 'Graham,' I patronised, 'you don't realise, we're not in exile any more. We don't need to sing songs of lament because Jesus died on the cross, remember, and brought us home. We are now his people, we are Christians.' I sat back and waited for him to catch on.

'Who told you that?' he replied.

I looked confused.

'Who told you that we were no longer in exile? Who said there are no laments to be sung to God? Are we really at home, with all the pain, turmoil, killings and hatred in the world? Is there nothing to lament about before God? Is there nothing to cry out? Is there no intercession we can make in our worship? And even if we can't sing songs of lament in our worship for ourselves, surely we ought to be bringing to God the pain of the world in our worship.'

What had we missed? We had ignored the value of intercession, the power of bringing the imperfections of the world before God and asking him to move.

Having said that, on one level, we don't want to go too far down that road because God is ultimately good, whether we feel like it or not. We need to remember to maintain a sense of balance in our worship. Like David and the psalmists, we need to be able to be brutally honest with God about the things that trouble us, as well as to be able to acknowledge his goodness and power. At times we may not feel at all like worshipping, and it is at those times that it is most important that we get on with the business of exercising our faith. That's worshipping in reality, and worship is supposed to reflect life.

And so we come to the practical challenge of working out how we actually can manage to worship God at the same time as being 100 per cent honest and faithful. How do we marry pain with praise? I think we've got a lot of work to do on that. At Soul Survivor Watford, we've been trying to explore some of this ground, at least endeavouring to understand a little more, even if we're not quite at the solution stage yet. When we have tried to learn about intercession in worship, fresh songs have arrived, and many have captured the spirit of the time. But I think we've got a long way to go to ensure that it remains God-centred as well as expressing our frustrations.

I have a strange feeling that we can learn much on this topic from the period in David's life after he killed Uriah the Hittite, Bathsheba's husband (after he had slept with her). The Lord sent the prophet Nathan to David to ask what he had done. David repented bitterly. Later, his child, born as a result of the affair, became ill, and the Lord said he was going to take him from David. David spent days weeping, mourning and refusing to eat. He called out to God in intercession, and the servants, when eventually the boy died, didn't know how to tell him because they were worried about how he might react. David saw them talking and asked the servants if the boy had died. 'He has, my Lord,' they answered. With that, David washed his face, got dressed and went to worship. As the servants stared on in disbelief, David explained that there was no point in mourning any longer, God's will had been done.

Depending on your point of view, David's reaction is, at first glance, either commendable or contemptible. Throughout the passage, David continually placed himself in a position of submission, reminding God that he was in control. He knew that God's decision would be final, and, perhaps more importantly, that it would be just. Despite the pain and sorrow it caused him, David was willing to trust God and accept his decision. As soon as his son died, David was back worshipping God. There was no bitterness, there were no recriminations, just supplication and trust. As he worshipped, we can imagine that he must have done so with a broken heart, the weeping and mourning were certainly no spectator show. If there was a place for David to worship God in his despair, then surely it must be worth our while exploring the possibilities?

During that first conversation in Cambridge, Graham talked about how as God's people, we need to be saying, 'Oh God, where are you?' Even if we are not doing that for our own situations, we should be doing it on behalf of a hurt and broken world. When it comes to worship, how self-indulgent it is for us to come and to say, 'Forget everything out there, let's just sing our happy songs.' How dare we keep it all for ourselves? When we come to worship, of course we need to rejoice, to praise and to give thanks, but we also need to make space to bring our intercessions and our songs of lament.

In many of the psalms we can see just that attitude. Even in the psalms of lament there is an 'I'm-going-to-be-honest-about-how-I-feel-about-this' attitude. Psalm 77 carries the sentiment, 'Oh Lord, it hurts, yet will I remember your past deeds, yet will I praise you, yet I will look to you.' Sometimes our worship is too much like a quick fix.

In search of my own quick fix of escapism, junk food and sun I went to California. Walk through the doors of Disneyland and you are in the land of magic and joy, where you can forget the cares you had at home. It's all suddenly so bright and fluffy and wonderful. Mickey's smiling and that's all that counts. Never having been there before I was surprised at the sense of déjà vu that had settled down in my head. Then I realised: it was just like church. Sometimes we come through the doors and think it is a place where we can forget the cares of the world. All those problems and pains are whisked away in a soufflé of happy lives and good teeth. It doesn't matter that our hearts are breaking; gloss it over with a few fast songs and reality need never be an issue. That's wrong. When we come in worship we come with all that we are and all that we have – if we gloss, squash or numb any part, then our worship is fake. Worship is bringing who we are to him; worship should be an expression of life.

The Hebrews didn't suffer quite so badly in this department. They didn't divide life into sacred and secular, into the things of the world and the things of the spirit. That attitude is the legacy of Greek philosophy, inspired by Plato and his pals. The 'Sunday Christian' thing is simply not a biblical concept. One of the words that is used in the Old Testament for worship literally means to work. That doesn't mean to work in the temple or to work in church, it means to work. That's right, they saw room for worship in the middle of farming, making, fixing and creating. Applied to today's job market we have a scenario where worship can be expressed through the medium of anything from recruitment consultancy to hairdressing. For the Jews, their understanding was that the whole of life should be an act of worship. Whether we are an industry fat cat or a blue collar underling, it's all a celebration of life and it's all a communication, a communion with God.

That's why Jewish culture valued as acts of worship the tearing of clothes as much as the banging of a tambourine. Here in the UK Church of today we still bang the tambourines, but we seem to have lost the torn clothes. The expressions of sorrow must be reintroduced to our communion with God, as they are part of the blueprint of our souls. Who would dream of chastising a parent as they mourn the loss of their teenage son? But when did we last sing a song that would be of real help in the situation? True, God's light does transcend pain, it does shine in the darkness, but it also illuminates the pain of the cross. It is good for us to say, 'Yet I will rejoice in the Lord,' but that 'yet' can only really come after we have told the Lord exactly where we are. That is faith. It's about coming to him in reality. It's praising him through the tears, not pretending that the tears aren't there.

If prophecy is revealing whatever is on God's heart, then you can be pretty sure that God's heart is, among other things, in mourning for all the lost. After all, didn't Jesus put them at the top of our 'to do' list before he went back to heaven? Worship is, as we have already established, a two-way process; we hang out with God, and in turn, are transformed and affected by his very nature. It therefore seems clear that our worship is missing out on something if we don't step in line with God's attitudes to the lost. Worship and prayer can become fused here, both being used to bend God's ear and knock on his door on behalf of our neighbours.

So What Does It Look Like?

Since we got put back on course with this, different songs have come up through Soul Survivor that have helped to express how we feel. The titles hint at this ('Can a nation be changed?' and 'Knocking on the door of heaven', to name two), and the general tone is one of 'Hey Lord, this is the state of your world, we call out to you and yet we praise you'. Prophetic intercession, I believe, is an aspect of worship. It should come out of the lifestyle of worship, the day to day that the Hebrews found so compatible with their faith.

Where better to turn than Ezekiel 4, where we find an adventure of one of God's craziest prophets. I don't know about you, but sometimes when I read the Bible (because I'm learning to have an enquiring mind), I train my mind to ask questions. I used to read the Bible, denouncing the bits that I didn't understand as irrelevant. There used to be passages in Ezekiel where I would repeatedly think, '?' My eyes would be permanently glazed and it was only a matter of time before I would drop the Word and pick up the TV remote to help bring me back to reality. Thankfully I've grown up a bit since then, and because of that, I've found much more in the book of Ezekiel than I had ever bargained for.

The Lord told Ezekiel, 'Now, son of man, take a clay tablet, put it in front of you and draw the city of Jerusalem on it.' So he drew: there's the temple, there are some houses, there's the mountain, there are some clouds in the sky, and there's a little bit of grass there. 'Then lay siege to it: Erect siege works against it, build a ramp up to it, set up camps against it and put battering rams around it' (vv. 1–2). Then he had to get a little model war going, make battering rams, a ramp, find something to represent the soldiers. It appears that this was not in the privacy of his back room.

We're talking 100 per cent public . . . 'Hello Ezekiel, what are you doing?' his neighbours may have asked.

'I'm drawing the city of Jerusalem on this clay tablet.'

'What are you doing now, Ezekiel?'

'I'm laying siege to Jerusalem. I have built my battering rams.'

'I can see that.'

'And here's my ramp and my siege works and my soldiers.'

'That's nice, Ezekiel.'

'Then, take an iron pan and place it as an iron wall between you and the city and turn your face towards it. It will be under siege, and you shall besiege it. This will be a sign to the house of Israel' (v. 3). If you want my opinion, that was a sign that Ezekiel had finally gone foot-chewingly mad. But it gets worse, we get onto the real nutty stuff . . .

'Then lie on your left side and put the sin of the house of Israel upon yourself. You are to bear their sin for the number of days that you lie on your side. I have assigned you the same number of days as the years of their sin. So for 390 days you will bear the sin of the house of Israel.' (vv. 4–5)

Now, just so that we understand this next bit, God tells Ezekiel to lie on his side. Lie down in front of the clay tablet with Jerusalem on it, with the siege works. Lie down and put the sin of Israel on you. Right, now you're to lie there in front of Jerusalem a day for every year of Israel's sin: 390 days, representing 390 years. So Ezekiel lies on his left side in front of the clay tablet for 390 days. That's over a year. That's a long time. He misses Christmas and his birthday, too. Again, the neighbours come by:

'Hello Ezekiel, what are you doing?'

'Ah, I'm lying in front of the city of Jerusalem.'

'But you were besieging it yesterday.'

'Yes, well I am lying in front of it and the sin of Israel is upon me.'

'Oh.'

'Yes, and I'm here for another year.'

And then he has to lie on his other side for the number of days that Judah has sinned, and that's forty, just over a month. And when he's done that for 390 days and then forty days, the Lord says, 'Turn your face toward the siege of Jerusalem and with bared arm prophesy against her' (v. 7). Now what does that mean? Jerusalem was under siege from her enemies, and God sets him up for a prophetic act. There can be real drama in prophecy, and this is Oscar material. We are told that he stands 'with bared arm' and prophesies against Jerusalem. After he had been lying on it for 390 days, can you imagine what his arm must have been like? Can you envisage the pain? (Exactly how much of this story is symbolic, I don't know, but we take it, for teaching purposes, at face value.) As he spoke, he wouldn't have opted for the soft and gentle approach, the one that goes, 'Well, Israel, you have been naughty boys and girls, haven't you? The Lord said he's not very pleased.

You'd better do better next time.' And 'Oh well, I've done that prophecy, I'd best go on to the next place.' I don't think that he did that. I think that after lying there for 390 days, when he lifted up his arm in agony, he didn't just prophesy God's words, he prophesied God's heart. He felt God's pain. That is what prophetic intercession is all about, and it's part of worship.

Another example of how prophetic intercession reveals the heart and pain of God can be found in the story of Hosea. God tells him to take the prostitute Gomer as his wife. God also tells him that she will be unfaithful to him, but that Hosea is to love, care for and treasure her as he would the most faithful of wives. She, God helpfully illustrates, will be his wife, but she will go with other men and she will lift up her skirts to every passing stranger. She will break his heart. Once this has gone according to plan, God tells Hosea to go and say to Israel, 'Israel, you are like a prostitute. I have been a faithful husband to you, Israel, and you have broken my heart because you've lifted up your skirts to every passing God.' When Hosea prophesied, even the expert theologians find it hard to tell, studying the book of Hosea, which bit is Hosea speaking and which bit is God. God told Hosea to take this prostitute so that when he prophesied the words had maximum force. It was both a visual representation and a spiritual revelation.

I'll never forget this story that John Wimber told years ago. He was speaking at a camp when a pastor friend of his told John that there was a woman in the church who said she had a prophecy for him. John Wimber said to his friend, 'Yeah, right. She's probably just single, in her late forties and in need of affirmation.' His friend replied that she was all of those things, but she also was usually pretty good at hearing God. So this woman came up to him and he said, 'Well, lady, go on, I hear you have a prophecy for me.' The woman burst into tears and started crying. John Wimber thought, 'Oh no, here we go, I've got an emotional female.' After a while he got fed up and said, 'Listen, lady, I'm a busy man. I don't know what your problem is, but can you tell me the prophecy and then we can get going.' She was sobbing her heart out. Then she looked up at him through her tears and she said, 'That's the prophecy.' It was as though a knife had gone through John Wimber's heart because suddenly he saw that God was crying over him. God was broken-hearted over him, over his sin, over his brokenness, over his pride and over his arrogance. He said he walked into the woods and he cried back. It changed his life. And all it was, was a woman crying, but they were God's tears.

When Hosea spoke to Israel about how they had prostituted themselves to every passing God, his agony was God's agony and it spoke to Israel. When Ezekiel bared his arm, he felt God's pain. Sometimes God uses us in ways that we might not understand. Our logical brains can shield us from revelation. Our hearts are often not so well defended. It is from there that intercession comes. Don't get me wrong, there is a real value in quietly working through a list of people and situations in need of prayer. There is also a place for being doubled over on the floor, aching for God to do something. As it says in Romans 8, 'We do not know how to pray as we should but the Spirit intercedes for us with sighs and groans too deep for words.' Intercession can often take the form of sighs and groans too deep for words. Words are important but they are not the only way.

In our church in Watford we haven't learned very much about this yet, and I don't know how to get there, but even as I write it I am thinking that we have got to find a way. We have our praise and thanksgiving – both precious things – but we also have our intercession where we share something of God's heart and we allow him to break our hearts with the things that break his. That's biblical worship, and I believe that the closer we get to Jesus in and through our worship, the more we feel his pain.

It's a funny thing, but have you ever noticed how good we have become at covering up our pain? How the shock of sudden negative emotions can lead to a knee-jerk reaction of suppression and denial? We're not good with pain – after all, who wants to hang out with someone who is permanently miserable? But when we do that repression thing, we also succeed in taking the edge off those decent emotions like joy and happiness. The people that I know who are truly alive are the ones who are not afraid of the pain as well as the joy.

I've got a friend called Pete Hughes who is a wonderful guy. We took him to South Africa in the summer and we left him there to be a youth worker on his year out in Port Elizabeth. The Hughes family are all big-hearted people who laugh a lot, but they also know how to feel the other stuff as well. Now Pete loves his friends so much that the process of leaving England was a big deal. At Heathrow when he said goodbye to everyone there were plenty of tears. Then in South Africa, it was the same situation when we left him in Port Elizabeth. It was a horrendous day; he was crying and I cried too. I was feeling so bad about it all, guilty that I was dumping him with all those strangers, and thinking the sorrow was in itself a terrible thing. For Pete, and for all his family, the pain is part of the joy. When you care a lot for people you can't feel great joy at seeing someone and not feel great sorrow when you don't see them, it doesn't work like that. That happens in our worship; when we have the great joy of knowing Jesus, he'll also break our hearts, he'll melt them so that we sense something of his pain for a hurting and broken world. That's why I love some of the Kevin Prosch songs – for their honesty. 'Oh break our hearts with the things that break yours.' What a line.

Another great song of Kevin's is 'How can I be satisfied?' The chorus carries the lines 'how can I be satisfied, unless you come near and stay by my side? . . . There has to be more Lord, there must be more . . .' Some have said that this should not be sung in worship because feeling far from God is not something to complain to God about; it's not his fault. While I understand this, I am sure that there is a recurrent theme of 'Where are you Lord?' throughout the Psalms. Whoever's fault it is – whether it be God's or ours – I want the Lord to hear my argument, and hear my cry for this world.

This is where it all comes together. My dream is about standing on the sidelines, watching as the lost are brought in. While we are not the bearers of salvation, we do play a part. Our songs can be that part. Somehow we've got to find a way of pulling it all together. We may not have discovered the whole truth yet, but the expression shouldn't be ignored.

7

Worship and Spiritual Warfare

One of the devil's major strategies is to deflect our attention from God and put it onto himself. It makes sense, doesn't it, that he would want to try to sever the link that exists between ourselves and our Maker? Assuming that, it therefore makes sense that the greatest antidote that we have in our possession is worship. We counteract his attempts to distract us by going deeper with God. The devil hates it when we worship because when we do we are focusing on God, fulfilling the promise that we were created with. What's more, I also believe that when we worship, battles are won in the heavenly places. Things get changed when we worship. Jesus said he came to proclaim and usher in the Kingdom. The devil will do all he can to prevent the rule of God being exercised on earth. When we worship we acknowledge the King of the Kingdom and as such the dynamic rule of God advances. Worship, I believe, is the supreme weapon of our warfare. It is the Christians' nuclear bomb.

The story of King Jehoshaphat is told in 2 Chronicles 20. We read,

> Some men came and told Jehoshaphat, 'A vast
> army is coming against you from Edom, from
> the other side of the Sea. It is already in
> Hazazon Tamar (that is En Gedi).' Alarmed,
> Jehoshaphat resolved to enquire of the Lord
> and he proclaimed a fast for all of Judah. The
> people of Judah came together to seek help
> from the Lord, indeed they came from every
> town in Judah to seek him. (vv. 2–4)

This reaction to the threat of attack, this unanimous
decision to fall to their knees, is one of the most
inspired examples of faith and humility in the Old
Testament. And sure enough, it paid off: 'Then the
Spirit of the Lord came upon Jahaziel son of Zechar-
iah, son of Benaiah, the son of Jeiel, the son of
Mattaniah, a Levite and descendant of Asaph, as he
stood in the assembly' (v. 14).

Notice the attention to the family history. It is not
only there to add a little colour to the characters, it
also sheds some important biographical light on the
proceedings. Jahaziel's Great Great Great Grand-
father was a Levite, which means that he was a priest
and the equivalent of a worship leader. Asaph was one
of the most famous worship leaders in all of Israel. He
was around at the time of David, King of Israel, and
clearly had passed something down through the gen-
erations. In verse 15 Jahaziel speaks:

> He said, 'Listen, King Jehoshaphat and all who
> live in Judah and Jerusalem! This is what the
> Lord says to you: "Do not be afraid or
> discouraged because of this vast army. For the

battle is not yours, but God's. Tomorrow march
down against them. They will be climbing up by
the Pass of Ziz, and you will find them at the
end of the gorge in the Desert of Jeruel. You
will not have to fight this battle. Take up your
positions; stand firm and see the deliverance
the Lord will give you, O Judah and Jerusalem.
Do not be afraid; do not be discouraged. Go
out to face them tomorrow, and the Lord will
be with you.'' ' (vv. 15–17)

When you think about it, that is an amazing statement.
There were three armies rolled into one vast one.
They seemed huge and guaranteed to wipe the floor
with Jehoshaphat's crew. But what does the Lord say?
'Relax – it's not your battle.'

I know how I would respond to such chilled-out
advice, and it would not be the way Jehoshaphat did it
in verse 18: 'Jehoshaphat bowed with his face to the
ground and all the people of Judah and Jerusalem fell
down in worship before the Lord.' Full marks for that
reaction. It sparked more of the same from some
others gathered around, and some Levites from the
Kohathites and Korahites stood up and praised the
Lord, the God of Israel, with 'a very loud voice'. The
loud voice seemed to help, reinforcing the faith-levels
like the roar of a lion. It puts fear into the enemies
round about. Lately God's Church has been learning
how to worship with a loud voice too.

Then,

Early in the morning they left for the Desert of
Tekoa. As they set out, Jehoshaphat stood and

said, 'Listen to me, Judah and people of
Jerusalem! Have faith in the Lord your God and
you will be upheld; have faith in his prophets
and you will be successful.' After consulting the
people, Jehoshaphat appointed men to sing to
the Lord and to praise him for the splendour of
his holiness as they went out at the head of the
army, saying: 'Give thanks to the Lord, for his
love endures forever.' (vv. 20–1)

What happened? Jehoshaphat put worshippers at the
head of the army. The men were there to praise God
for the splendour of his holiness so that as the army
was going to fight, it really would be God's battle. They
praised God by singing, 'Give thanks to the Lord, for
his love endures forever.'

Then in verse 22, 'As they began to sing and praise,
the Lord set ambushes against the men of Ammon
and Moab and Mount Seir who were invading Judah,
and they were defeated.' While Israel worshipped,
God rolled up his sleeves and won the battle. It seems
that the enemies fought amongst themselves to the
extent that 'When the men of Judah came to the place
that overlooks the desert and looked towards the vast
army, they saw only dead bodies lying on the ground;
no-one had escaped' (v. 24).

Sometimes when things are tough, when we don't
know what else to do, we think that our enemy, our
circumstances are like a vast army ranged against us.
At those times the greatest weapon we have is worship.
Praising him in the midst of our difficulties, saying to
God that we believe the battle is his rather than ours,
can be the catalyst for what are truly signs and won-

76

ders. The deal is the same as God offered Jehoshaphat: we worship, he fights. Whatever circumstances
we might be up against, we can always trust in him.

We see the same principle at work in the Acts of the
Apostles when Paul and Silas were jailed at Philippi.
They had been arrested and put into prison, held in
chains in the deepest dungeon. At midnight, instead
of sleeping or complaining or trying to escape, they
worshipped God with no holds barred. 'By coincidence' an earthquake just happened to be brewing,
and as it rattled the prison, their door flew open and
their chains fell off. The good stuff didn't just stop
there, as the jailer and his family all came to know
Jesus. With God fighting the battle they had no need
of their own strategies or implements. Worship was
enough; God did the rest.

In this context worship and praise build faith. When
we look solely at the circumstances that are worrying
us, then they can overwhelm us. But when we give
thanks and recount the reasons why we can be thankful to God, then those things build faith in us and we
begin to believe what we are saying.

There are many Christians who seem to be locked
up in prisons of their own making. If only, instead of
looking at the problems they would turn to worship
and praise, then their prison doors would open, their
own chains would fall away. We need to use praise as a
spiritual weapon against the enemy. It is so much
more healthy than spending lots of time talking to the
enemy, rebuking him and telling him off. We're not
meant to be doing too much of that hand to hand
stuff; leave it to God. We want to put our attention
where it belongs: on Jesus Christ.

8

Creativity in Worship

Picture this: at some point, back in the time before there was time, there was God: Father, Son and Holy Spirit. The three of them were there, just being, existing and doing whatever God-like things they did. This was the time before the universe existed, and I like to imagine that the Father would often say to the Son and to the Holy Spirit, 'Son, Holy Spirit, I love you. You're fantastic.' Perhaps the reply would come back from the Son, 'Father, you're great. Holy Spirit, you're amazing.' 'Father, Son,' the Holy Spirit may have said, 'I'm so pleased to be part of you. I'm so happy to be together.'

And so it went on: Father, Son and Holy Spirit together as the ultimate harmonious family unit. At one particular point in non-time, I imagine that the Father cleared his non-throat, and addressed the other two. (While I'm not usually that concerned about accuracy, I believe that we can safely assume here that it was the Father that would have brought this point up.)

'Hey,' he might have begun, 'you know how we love each other so much?' Murmurs of agreement from the other two.

79

'Well, why don't we make something like us that we can bestow our love upon?'

'Yes,' may have come the agreement, 'with so much love around, it seems a shame to let it go to waste.'

'What a fantastic idea!' the Holy Spirit may have chipped in. 'Shall I go and do it?'

And so, after six days (or six chunks of time, depending on your politics), there was the earth with everything in it. The Bible kind of carries the story from here on in, but it's interesting to note that the very first thing we know about God from Genesis 1 is that he likes to create. Having got that one sorted, it then becomes clear that we too, being made in his image, have a natural desire and ability to create, reflecting the nature of our Maker.

Think about a man and a woman. Pretty soon in many relationships, the subject of sex comes up. Now apart from being fun, sex is also about procreation. It is a mirror of what went on in heaven before time began; it is the joining of two people to create something like them. At its best, the motivation for starting a family is a desire to share a discovered love with another individual. We share God's instincts in this sense. We were made in his image.

And so it does not take a genius to work out that God wants us to worship him creatively. Throughout the Old Testament the commands to worship come thick and fast. Many of the worship festivals can only be imagined in widescreen. At many key points in Israel's history they celebrated, dedicated or mourned in spectacular ways.

We do not see many pictures of congregational worship in the New Testament. If we are looking for a model for worship where better to look than heaven? The best picture of creative worship I can find is the glimpse we get of the worship of heaven as seen in Revelation chapters 4 and 5.

> After this I looked, and there before me was a door standing open in heaven. And the voice I had first heard speaking to me like a trumpet said, 'Come up here, and I will show you what must take place after this.' At once I was in the Spirit, and there before me was a throne in heaven with someone sitting on it. (4:1–2)

Then John begins to build the picture: 'There before me was a throne . . . with someone sitting on it. And the one who sat there had the appearance of jasper and carnelian' (4:3). That means it was colourful. 'A rainbow, resembling an emerald, encircled the throne' (4:3). So there's the colourful character on the throne, there's the rainbow – containing the spectrum of all known colours – encircling the throne. 'Surrounding the throne were twenty-four other thrones and seated on them were twenty-four elders. They were dressed in white and had crowns of gold on their heads' (4:4). Now these chiefs, dressed in white, were not, I take the liberty of assuming, dressed in a shade of dull white of the ancient towel variety. No, these boys were gleaming, reflecting all the colour that was already in the room. As if that wasn't enough, they were wearing golden crowns on their heads, just to add a tad more in the way of brightness. 'From the throne came flashes of lightning, rumblings and peals of thunder' (4:5). So you can imagine it: there's the throne, really colourful, rainbow all around, then from the throne flashes of lightning and peals of thunder continually pulsate. The elders are doing their bit too, making sure that the spectacle is fully panoramic.

'Before the throne seven lamps were blazing. These are the seven spirits of God. Also before the throne there was what looked like a sea of glass, clear as crystal' (4:5–6). So we now add seven blazing lamps and beneath them a sea of glass, which would have reflected and magnified all of this colour. About time to put the sunglasses on?

> In the centre, around the throne, were four
> living creatures, and they were covered with
> eyes, in front and behind. The first living
> creature was like a lion, the second was like an
> ox, the third had a face like a man, the fourth
> was like a flying eagle. Each of the four living
> creatures had six wings and was covered with
> eyes all around, even under his wings. (4:6–8)

And here comes the worship,

> Day and night they never stopped saying,
> 'Holy, holy, holy is the Lord God Almighty,
> who was, and is, and is to come.' Whenever
> the living creatures give glory, honour and
> thanks to him who sits on the throne and who
> lives for ever and ever, the twenty-four elders
> fall down before him who sits on the throne,
> and worship him who lives for ever and ever.
> They lay their crowns before the throne, and

say, 'You are worthy, our Lord and God, to
receive glory and honour and power, for you
created all things, and by your will they were
created and have their being.' (4:8–11)

Now just imagine the picture. There are the four
living creatures, and whenever they sing their song
the twenty-four elders leap up from their thrones, fall
down before the big throne, toss their crowns down
and say, 'You are worthy, our Lord and God.' Then
someone presses the automatic repeat button and the
matinee performance spills over to the evening. The
creativity of colour, movement and voices is enough to
make Andrew Lloyd-Webber weep.

The point of all this is that it proves that God loves
the exercise of the creative. Yet he doesn't love
creativity for the sake of creativity. All of that stuff
with thunder, lightning, elders, living creatures and
crowns seems to me like a prelude to the actual
climax, something that, in itself, is even more fantastic
and inspired. And here it is . . .

Then I saw in the right hand of him who sat
on the throne, a scroll with writing on both
sides and sealed with seven seals. And I saw a
mighty angel proclaiming in a loud voice,
'Who is worthy to break the seals and open the
scroll?' But no-one in heaven or on earth or
under the earth could open the scroll or even
look inside it. I wept and wept because no-one
was found who was worthy to open the scroll
or look inside. Then one of the elders said to
me, 'Do not weep! See, the Lion of the tribe

of Judah, the Root of David, has triumphed.
He is able to open the scroll and its seven
seals. (5:1–5)

On one level this section carries a strong symbolic
meaning, but at the same time, it is good to imagine
the picture. John sees a scroll, yet there is not a single
person or creature in heaven or earth to open it or
even look inside. John wrote that he wept because of
this, but was comforted by an angel who said, 'Don't
weep, for there is someone.'

Here we go; hold tight. The trumpets start to
blow. The curtain opens and there's a big introduc-
tion for the triumphant Lion of the tribe of Judah,
the Root of David. Naturally you would expect the
Lion to make an appearance at this point, but
instead the curtain opens and what do we see? A
lamb. It's not even a particularly feisty-looking lamb.
In fact, John comments that it looks as though it has
been slain. It stands in the centre of the throne
encircled by the four living creatures and all the
elders. What a picture. The Lion of Judah, the
ultimate symbol of power and *deliverance*, is the dying
lamb, Jesus Christ.

We are told through all this that right at the heart of
worship, amidst the most outrageous bursts of creativity, is Jesus. At the heart of it all is his act of atoning
sacrifice. We don't worship the creativity, nor do we
worship the worship. Instead, we look to the blood-
soaked corpse of Christ and remember what it's all
about.

As the blood drips from the saving Lamb, all the
players worship. Once the scroll has been taken, the

four living creatures and twenty-four elders fall down before the Lamb, each holding a harp and a golden bowl full of incense. These, we are told, are the prayers of the saints, the offering that you and I give to the Lord. Together they sang a new song, 'You are worthy to take the scroll . . .' (5:9).

> Then I looked and heard the voice of many
> angels numbering thousands upon thousands,
> and ten thousand times ten thousand. They
> encircled the throne of the living creatures
> and the elders. In a loud voice they sang,
> 'Worthy is the Lamb, who was slain, to
> receive power and wealth and wisdom and
> strength and honour and glory and praise!'
> (5:11–12)

What started with a relatively small cast – a handful of beasts and a few suited elders – soon begins to swell in size. In come the angels, 'ten thousand times ten thousand', or so many as to make counting an impossible task. They circled the throne, as well as the living creatures and the elders. Then they began to sing. Loudly. Can you imagine the volume? It would be like filling Wembley Stadium with proud mothers, all watching their sons score the winning goal for the FA cup. Yet there is one thing missing: 'Then I heard every creature in heaven and on earth and under the earth and on the sea, and all that is in them, singing: "To him who sits on the throne and to the Lamb, be praise and honour and glory and power, for ever and ever!" ' (5:13). And there we are. Literally. The 'every creature' includes us!

The finish is almost comical, as the four living creatures say 'Amen' (reminding me of dozing politicians as they chip in with their mumbled 'hear hear'). The final response is for the elders to fall over.

Depending on where you come from, Revelation isn't one of the most preached about books. It seems to me that often the colour and creativity, the sheer commitment and passion of the cast make the book seem somewhat inaccessible for us in church. Can you imagine dressing your elders up in a little white and gold ensemble and getting them to fall down on cue? Yet one day you and I will be taking up our places in the cast of thousands. Doesn't it make sense to try and get a little practice in first?

When it comes to leading worship here on earth, Revelation 4 and 5 offer us an indispensable guide. If we can truly imbibe these pictures, if we can somehow absorb them and allow them to influence our times of worship, then those times will surely offer a greater connection with heaven itself. And while I may have been a bit flippant when I suggested that we might fancy getting a few practice rounds under our belts before we get called up for an eternity of the real thing, worship will be our main function in heaven. You don't see much in the way of education, relaxation, work or sport in John's vision of heaven. What you see is wall to wall worship. I'm not sure if there will be transport in heaven, nor am I sure if we'll have specific work to do, but you can be sure that whatever we do, worshipping God will play a major part in every aspect of our eternal lives.

Recently I went to see an amazing group of percussionists called 'Stomp' perform in London. It was a really creative spectacle. There were eight people in this show, and for roughly two hours they did nothing more than bang things. Not just any type of things, mind, these were hand picked. They used kitchen sinks, dustbins, newspapers, brooms, matchboxes, car bonnets and all sorts of things. As we sat and watched, the performance started with one person coming on stage to sweep the floor. Then someone else came on and started beating out a different rhythm with another broom. More people joined them and developed the music until there were eight people, each with brooms, creating a fantastic noise.

I suddenly realised the creativity that could be unleashed by the simplest of instruments. That sort of creativity is what we can bring to God as our worship. We need to be creative to please God – he is, after all, a little on the creative side himself – by using the gifts that he's given us. It's not about being creative in the first instance to make a good impression on others, it's to express our devotion through the creativity. We have learnt so much from many creative people, such as Kevin Prosch, who's taught us about rhythm and about pushing against the barriers of tradition. We have also learned plenty from other people that we have met from different places. I remember the friends we made in a Zulu township in South Africa who do incredible things simply with their voices.

The 'Stomp' show reminded me that creativity is God-given. It exists within each of us – not just the rich, the ethnic, the educated, the broken or the Greek. It is up to the Church to find ways of allowing people to unite their worship and their creativity. It is up to us as individuals to find ways of using our own talents to worship God. In many churches we are still living solely off the creativity of people who died over four hundred years ago. There are so many ways we can release the creative gifts in the Church to find their expression in worship today. Why not encourage the painters and sculptors to create works of art which will give us visions of Jesus, the dancers to help us to express worship with our bodies? We can be so creative in our use of light (we've even started using candles at Soul Survivor Watford!) and different instruments. We have had some wonderful worship times recently when all our drummers and percussionists have played together. At a recent Soul Survivor we had fifteen drummers playing on stage at once. Then we have had meetings when there have been no instruments at all.

Of course there are dangers within this. Worship was never meant to be about performance, nor was it meant to bring glory to those involved (apart from God, that is). Whether you are exploring worship through art, silence or cuisine the principles are the same: do it for God, make it accessible, be prepared to hold back on the creative genius if necessary to help others get closer to God. Above all, make sure that your public worship is mirroring what you do in private.

I'll never forget John Wimber's testimony. At one point, before he had become a Christian, he was walking through Times Square in New York. Approaching him was a religious nutter wearing a sandwich board, bearing the slogan 'I'm a fool for Christ'. 'Yup,' thought John, 'you certainly are.' As the old man walked past him, John saw what was written on the back of the board: 'Whose fool are you?' This was enough to get John thinking. If we're going to be fools, who better than Jesus to be fools for?

I want to give my all to him. I want to give my pride, my energy, my gifts and my failings. I don't want to hold onto anything. Creativity in worship is about using everything we have to tell God how wonderful he is. It is also about focusing directly on the Lamb of God, Jesus himself, and dedicating our lives to him.

9

For the Audience of One

Let's be honest; the Church in western Europe, including the UK, is still dying. Downsizing, dieting or shaping up, whatever way you want to put it, the Church is shrinking. This is happening despite the best efforts of the Toronto blessings, the Pensacola outbreak, the New Cell Revolution and the rise of deliverance ministry. All these things, these shiny things that many of us in the Church have thought of as God's marketing strategy, have made little impact on the exodus. All comers, from social commentators to statisticians have noted such a decline, and I have to agree with them. Even in my corner of England, a place where many a radical teaching has been made palatable and user-friendly, the numbers have been coming down. Over a period of fourteen years, groups that used to be regularly packed with fifty young people have got used to accommodating numbers half that amount. As an added shock, I'm not talking about groups from old school churches, but evangelical and even (wait for it) evangelical charismatic churches. Yes, that's right, those churches where we know about signs, wonders and the power of the Playstation are chucking them out as fast as the ones where the coffee rota is written in Latin. Maybe the Holy Spirit doesn't seem to be there enough or perhaps we're doing it all wrong; the truth is plain and simple, and each year there have been fewer young people in our churches than the last. Something needs to happen, and there's no point pretending that things aren't bad; they are.

Many preachers have lately been partial to a bit of socio-scriptural labelling. We've heard that this is the Joshua generation – a claim born out by the similarities between Joshua, assistant to Moses, and the current generation who have a similar potential. Others have plumped for the suggestion that we are the Gideon generation – drawing on the similarities between the warrior who started out afraid and the group of people that some like to label Generation X. Not long ago I even heard that this is the Abraham, Isaac and Jacob generation. I can't remember why, but the presence of three characters had me pretty convinced that it was correct. Not wanting to be left out, I make my own recommendation: this is the Samuel generation.

Owning Up

Samuel was Hannah's son. The beginning of the book of Samuel shows her to be in great distress as she is barren. Her urge to have a child isn't simply a slightly intense brand of broodiness, but a desperate desire to avoid the stigma of childlessness. 'In bitterness of soul Hannah wept much and prayed to the Lord' (1 Samuel 1:10). She was ashamed of her barrenness, and she went to the temple to pour out her heart to

God. She didn't go there to pretend everything was great, nor did she go there to try and forget about her problems. She went to the temple to tell God how she felt.

This type of honesty is something that has been cropping up in the Church lately. As we follow the story of Samuel the value of such truthfulness will become clearer. We need to be honest with God and with each other; just like Hannah, we need to face up to the fact that we are part of a barren Church. The Church does a lot of things, but it is not really doing great things in the realms of baby production.

The Alpha course is doing great things in evangelism. However, the one age group which even Alpha is finding it difficult to reach in significant numbers is the teenagers. As far as that generation is concerned, the Church is not creating life. While there are a few isolated pockets of activity, in general the Church is coming round to realise that it is barren. As far as I can see, that realisation is the Church's first sign of progress.

Many of our churches have, until recently, ignored the crisis, either because they have not known what to do or because they haven't cared. In my own church, the Church of England, much of the decay has been covered up by money. If it wasn't for the fact that the Anglican bank balance is so healthy (and I mean really healthy), the crisis would be impossible to ignore. As it is, the cash means that everything keeps on running smoothly. The trouble is that money is not representative of today's takings; instead it's dead people's money that was given long ago and has been wisely invested. Today's C of E is like a flaking multinational, whose past fortunes bail out the shortfalls of today. Of course, we don't measure the success of a church by its balance sheet; we measure the success of a church by the number of spiritual babies it produces and nurtures. Over the last five years the Church at large has been united by a common realisation that the current decline offers grave problems for the future. If we don't do something fast there will be no young people left. In most Anglican churches there aren't even any there right now. According to the Archbishop of Canterbury, more than half our Anglican churches are run without a youth work. Sadly the situation in many of the newer churches is the same. While there has been a distinct buzz about certain of their number which have grown dramatically, these churches are not indicative of a general trend where teenagers are concerned.

When I was in Norway recently, I heard a true story about the Bishop of Oslo, who had met with some of the church leaders I was visiting. They were surprised when he, a liberal, asked them to pray for him as he was so worried about the barren nature of the Church. Such expressions of unity and honesty are the first steps to a solution. Like Hannah, we need to see our shame and get down on our knees before God.

Hannah was desperate enough for a child that if God gave her a son, she promised that she would not own, control or try to keep him for herself. 'Lord,' she said, 'if you would grant me a son I will give him back to you.' God, I believe, is waiting for the Church to say those same things to him now. We need his Spirit in this generation, we need him to breathe life over the bones of the Church, we need him to use us to turn the hearts of this generation back to him. And when that happens, we must not try to control, manipulate or keep them for ourselves. We will have to allow them to be his people, not ours.

A Decent Education

I believe that God is going to do a new thing, that through our stepping out and by his grace, young people will again come into the Church. Hannah, when Samuel was born, kept her word and dedicated him to the Lord. She put him in the temple, where she would visit him once a year to give him new underwear and stuff like that. Through her dedication and sacrifice, Samuel grew up a unique and useful person. This dedication and sacrifice remains the key for our spiritual children; they too must grow up in the temple.

Samuel, we are told, served under Eli, the priest (1 Samuel 2:11). This struck me particularly as being relevant for all those churches like Soul Survivor, which started as youth churches or congregations. At times, there has been a tendency for these to start in rebellion, kicking back against the outdated structures of the Church. The trouble is, however, that for many of those that start in rebellion, they will end in rebellion too. Call it a genetic code. Therefore, in the same way that it was important for Samuel to grow up in the temple, so does the Samuel generation need to grow up in the full body of the Church. We must love and identify with the Church, and that means the whole Church.

Another significant factor in Samuel's childhood

was that he served under Eli the priest. Reading this you may be jumping ahead of me now, thinking, ah yes, Sammy grew up under the authority of a wise old priest and so we ought to find wise old priests of our own. Wrong. Eli was a prat. He was so self-indulgent that he died when he fell back in his chair and broke his neck. Like Samuel, we don't have a choice about the Church. We may well look at it and feel embarrassed, repulsed even, but being a Christian means being part of God's family, prats and all. Samuel grew up learning obedience and respect. I know that any self-respecting postmodernist would run a mile from the suggestion that we need a dose of these two character traits, but I'm afraid we can't avoid it.

So it wasn't all plain sailing in the temple. Eli's sons, Hophni and Phinehas, were sinners. In fact, verse 12 of chapter 2 describes them as 'wicked men' with 'no regard for the Lord'. They desecrated the house of God by having sex with girls at the entrance to the temple. But there's more:

> Now it was the practice of the priests with the
> people that whenever anyone offered a
> sacrifice and while the meat was being boiled,
> the servant of the priest would come with a
> three-pronged fork in his hand. He would
> plunge it into the pan or kettle or cauldron or
> pot, and the priest would take for himself
> whatever the fork brought up. This is how they
> treated all the Israelites who came to Shiloh.
> But even before the fat was burned, the
> servant of the priest would come and say to
> the man who was sacrificing, 'Give the priest

some meat to roast; he won't accept boiled meat from you, but only raw.'

If the man said to him, 'Let the fat be burned up first, and then take whatever you want,' the servant would then answer, 'No, hand it over now; if you don't, I'll take it by force.' (1 Samuel 2:13–16)

Permission to be confused. When I first read this, I failed to see how a bit of roast lamb was a bigger deal than having sex with maidens in the temple. In fact, and this may just be my own opinion, I would say that deciding to roast one's lamb in favour of boiling it is a sign of considerable style and taste. God, it would seem, does not agree: 'This sin of the young men was very great in the Lord's sight, for they were treating the Lord's offering with contempt' (1 Samuel 2:17). The deal with the offering indicated their selfish and disrespectful attitudes to God. The sin of sleeping with the maidens was really bad, but the meat theft remained the big sin. It was the common practice that the people of Israel would bring sacrifices to the Lord as part of their worship, just as we do today when we bring a sacrifice of praise. Sometimes the people had plenty, and sometimes they had little, but the principle of sacrifice remains the same for them and for us.

The people of Israel brought their lambs, doves, goats and whatever else was appropriate to the temple. The practice was that the meat would be boiled before it was burnt, making sure that all the fat had come away first. Priests didn't get paid in those days, and so to prevent starvation they were allowed to have a lucky dip when the meat was being boiled. This had the added advantage of entertaining the crowds as they were queuing up and waiting for their meat to be prepared. The priests or their servants were allowed to take a three-pronged fork (and for some reason it had to be a three-pronged fork), and they would plunge it once in the boiling water. Whatever attached itself to the fork was theirs to eat, while the rest would be sacrificed to the Lord.

Perhaps Eli's sons had short arms, but at some point it seems they decided that the one shot deal in the boiling water wasn't good enough for them. Instead they decided that they would allow themselves to grab whatever they wanted while it was still raw, and roast it to their individual tastes.

The big problem with this behaviour is that they were manipulating the worship of God into something that would be of benefit to themselves. And that is the biggest sin in the world: to touch the worship of God. It's what Satan got slung out of heaven for, and is the root of all our problems.

In the Church, we too are guilty of stealing God's worship. This might get you thinking of examples, and many of us would point the finger firstly at those who carry on with the old hymns choir that wear dresses. Oh my goodness, when will they learn and be like us? Being like us, though, can also mean being wrong. At times we declare that a worship session was irrelevant, doing nothing for us. Hello! Whoever said it was for us in the first place? Realising that the worship is all for God is a major step along the road to understanding Christianity. It is about us ministering to him, giving something back to the one who gave everything he had on the cross.

When we come to worship we shouldn't be checking out who's leading, writing off the service if it happens to be someone whose style we don't like. The same goes for the songs; complaining that a particular song is out of date and letting it put us off our worship shows that we have misunderstood the whole point of the thing. The heart of worship is that it's all about Jesus. Eli's sons missed it, and we need to be careful that we don't miss it also. That band up the front may seem about as tuneful and creative as a lump of boiled meat, but boiled meat is what we need to give.

There may be hundreds of reasons why you would want to leave your church. The worship may be slack, the teaching overly dry or the people out of touch. But think about Samuel; not only did he have to serve under Eli, but he was part of an institution that was corrupt and decayed in the most repulsive of ways. And what did Samuel do? He stayed there. He had died to himself and was living for God, living to be a faithful servant of his heavenly Master. We're not talking about a dry patch here; it was years before things got better. But all the same, Samuel remained faithful and holy.

Things Get Moving

By the time we get to chapter 3 of the first book of Samuel, God is getting involved. One night the Lord called Samuel, and he goes to find Eli, thinking it was him who called. Samuel didn't recognise God's voice, and he 'did not yet know the Lord: the word of the Lord had not yet been revealed to him'. Don't you find it incredible that he could grow up ministering to the Lord in the temple and yet the word of the Lord had not been spoken to him? In a sense, he didn't know the Lord. Isn't it frightening that we have people who grow up in the midst of the Church and don't know how to hear his voice, especially when Jesus said he is the Good Shepherd and his sheep hear his voice. These are days when we need to be desperately asking the Lord to speak.

Samuel finally sussed it out when Eli told him what to say. 'Speak to me, Lord,' he replied when the Lord next called him, 'for your servant is listening.' These are revealing words. I know that if I had been Samuel, I would have said, 'Listen, Lord, for your servant is speaking. And boy, has your servant got a lot to say to you.' But Samuel didn't do that, he said, 'Speak, Lord, for your servant is listening.'

My longing is that we become a Church that listens to the voice of the Lord. It seems to me that it was when he started to hear God that things really began to take off for Samuel. Firstly he was used by God to sort out Eli's sons. God told him to go and tell Eli that he and his sons had sinned greatly against God and that they would die as a result. Going to your boss and telling him that his sons are due for annihilation is bound to be a trifle nerve-racking. Samuel, however, was faithful, although understandably nervous.

'What was it he [the Lord] said to you?' Eli asked. 'Do not hide it from me. May God deal with you, be it ever so severely, if you hide from me anything he told you.' So Samuel told him everything, hiding nothing from him.

Then Eli said, 'He is the Lord; let him do what
is good in his eyes.' (vv. 17–18)

I believe that as God does a new thing with this
generation, he will give them words to speak to the
leadership of the Church. They may be tough words,
perhaps even on a par with Samuel's, and so it is vital
that they be rooted in the Church, and able to hear
God's voice clearly. The renewal of the Church will
come through the young people from within the
Church.

I heard a story about a youth group that came to our
Soul Survivor festival one year. They came from a very
traditional church, and most of them wouldn't even
have considered themselves Christians when they
arrived. During the festival God met with them and
he did some wonderful things. They went back to
their church and on their first Sunday back, the vicar
asked them if they wanted to share what happened to
them. As they started to say what had happened many
of the people in the congregation began to weep at
the change they could see in them. They heard their
children saying things that they never thought they'd
hear them say. One of the young people asked if they
could all pray for the rest of the church. They moved
along the pews, praying for the people, and it renewed
the church; it brought life. I had a letter from their
vicar, telling of how his church had been transformed.
He believed that it couldn't have happened any other
way.

The Samuel generation may not declare that people have to die, but they will surely point to things that
need radical change. That idea brings to mind my

'Things I Would Abolish in Church List' but it also conjures up a certain degree of fear. Deep down, I am sure that God will surprise me on this one. He's not so bothered about what I perceive as being the sins of the Church, but is probably more concerned with my personal, well ignored faults. And so we need to be ready to hear God's voice. He may say that it is time for some things to die that I want to stay as they are.

The Point of It All

Samuel's birth was miraculous. His childhood was something special and his role as receiver of God's word wasn't exactly mundane. He became a prophet to the nation of Israel – correction, he became *The* prophet to the nation of Israel. Why? What, you may ask, did such a great pedigree lead up to? The culmination of his life's work was this: one day God told him to go into a little town and to meet a guy with a lady's name, and to anoint his youngest son to be king of Israel. That was it. He went to Bethlehem, asked Jesse to show him his family, and poured a jug of olive oil over David's head. That was his life's mission, the high point of everything he did. Forgive my rudeness, but is that it? Was there nothing more significant, nothing more powerful? If it had been me, I would certainly have hesitated when it came to anointing David as king; surely a miraculous birth, chats with God and an upbringing in the temple trumped sheep and a few teenage songs written on a harp?

Perhaps part of our calling as the Samuel generation is to emulate this final characteristic. It seems crazy to talk about legacy in relation to people who have only just started shaving, but perhaps the glory may not be for us. God save us from trying to be something that we're not called to be, from trying to do something that we are not called to do. We have to encourage those that go after us. We need to make space for them. We need to pray for them, to anoint them, to bless them. We need to encourage them and to mentor them. We need to realise that we are a Samuel and not a David. What a tragedy it would have been if Samuel had refused to anoint David because of his own ambition. Samuel grew up hearing the voice of the Lord, and the event at Bethlehem was his biggest test. 'Are you in it for my purposes or are you in it for your own glory?' says the Lord. Humility, humility, humility.

My former boss and permanent friend, David Pytches was Bishop of Chile, Bolivia and Peru for thirteen years. He then came back to England, where he was Vicar of St Andrew's, Chorleywood, for nineteen years. While he was Vicar of St Andrew's, he started a festival called New Wine that has impacted many churches in this country. Seven and a half thousand people have been going to that festival just about every year since 1989. Soul Survivor the festival and everything else under the banner has come under his authority, and started with his permission. He's written books that have sold, unlike mine. In 1996 David retired as Vicar of St Andrew's, and since then on a Sunday, when he's not travelling, he sits near the front at our church in Watford. When he's not feeling too tired he comes and sits at the back in the evening service. When it comes to the ministry time, he's one of the first up the front to pray for people. Sometimes

I phone him up or I go round and I ask him how he thinks things are going. He usually says, 'Well now you ask, I do wonder about this' or 'I'm not sure you should be doing that . . .' But he usually ends up by saying, 'But you're the pastor, do whatever you think.' I pray to God that if I ever get to David's age, I will have half that humility. And it's not as if he doesn't care, he gets really excited when things go well and he gets quite upset when they don't go so well. It amazes me; he just comes to serve. David is someone who has learnt to be a Samuel.

In the early days, when we had just done our first Soul Survivor festival, we met a musician called Kevin Prosch and were very enamoured with him (and he is a great guy to be enamoured with). I went to David to ask permission to put together a week-long tour of gig venues with Kevin and his band. David asked me again and again if I was sure, that it all sounded very expensive and problematic. My charm won through in the end, and he gave it his support.

Well, I miscalculated. Kevin was fantastic but I booked halls that were too big, with a PA system that was too expensive. At the end of the week we had lost £15,000. It hurts even now to think about it. I was completely devastated. I went to David and offered my resignation. 'What are you talking about?' he said. 'First of all, I'm the boss; I made the final decision to do it. If anyone takes the blame it's me, not you. I was fully aware of the facts and I said to do it, so you've got nothing to worry about.'

If it had gone well, and we hadn't lost £15,000, I know from other experiences that David wouldn't have said, 'I'm the boss, I made the final decision.

Let my name go on the press release.' David would have kept completely quiet.

I want to be that kind of Samuel. I believe that God is calling us all to be like that, to have a generous heart that cares more for his purposes than for our personal glory. I want to be real in my worship of God. I want to give him the honour and glory that's due his name. I want to be in a place where I can hear his voice. I want to play a part in God's masterplan. Do you?

10

The Worship Leader's File

1. *How to Be a Worship Leader Without Being a Donkey*

The following could lose me many friends if I don't explain myself first. I really like worship leaders. Some of them are my best friends. The following is written tongue-in-cheek and the aim is not to patronise or insult but to encourage and affirm. So this is to all you donkeys out there with love from me.

There seem to be two similarities that unite people who get up and lead us in worship. First, many of them are very good at getting the spiritual things right. They often have an ability to respond to the prompting of the Holy Spirit and the mood of the meeting, steering things this way and that. Second, they can often be utter morons. Common sense and practical, logical thought seem to go out the window like last year's boy band. Not that having the brain of a particularly ingenious scout will necessarily make you into a champion worship leader, it's just that getting those things wrong can often hinder the anointing. And so, for those of you who are worship leaders, and for those of you who aren't but who like to tell those who are how to do it, I present the Soul Survivor guide to doing it (without being a donkey).

Before Leading, Think

What has God been saying to the group recently? What is the group thinking, worrying, rejoicing about? How can I reflect this in the choice of song? What does God want to say to the group? What do the other leaders think we should be focusing on? How do I prophetically address this in the choice of songs?

I think that the worship leader in a sense should be both pastor and prophet. As a pastor he/she should be asking during the days before a meeting: 'What is going on in the congregation that needs reflecting upon and needs to be expressed in worship?' It's an obvious point, but a recent bereavement can't go unnoticed in the worship. A seemingly endless stream of chirpy numbers when there is weeping and wailing all around could be classed as inappropriate. Times of repentance, rebuke, harmony and struggle are just a few of the many different circumstances that need to be reflected on from the front.

It's an example that I've used before, but Matt's song 'Coming back to the heart of worship' was a specific reaction to the tone of our church during the first few months of 1996. It was, and still is, a pastoral song, even more than it was a prophetic one. It expressed our feelings, and helped us through the transition of refining the way we worshipped. In worship we express; we bring our lives, we bring our concerns, our anxieties, our joys, our praises, our questions to God.

As prophet, the leader needs to be asking God for direction and inspiration. If the worship isn't inspired by God, if it hasn't started out with a desire for God to speak, then it's going to have a bit of a struggle as it progresses. From there on in, once the essential preparation has taken place, then the leader needs to be acting as both driver and navigator, trying to ascertain what's up ahead, and devising the best route to get there. So the worship leader here should be asking the prophetic question, 'Lord, where do you want to take us in the worship, what do you want to say?'

Choosing Songs

I don't know how many times I've been in a meeting where thousands have been singing along to 'Did You Feel the Mountains Tremble?' When the masses reach the bit in the song where it's their cue to cheer, the atmosphere is usually pure electricity. Yet, take the song back home and try to recreate it with a home-group of six and you end up with something closer to a glib whimper than the intended glorious cheer. In such a situation, I would suggest that the most appropriate course of action would not be to halt the meeting and individually interrogate all those present, forcing them to disclose their deep sin which has so hindered the worship. Instead, try using your head beforehand. Also, if there is only one male or female in the meeting and he or she does not sing in tune, then maybe lots of songs with male/female repeats aren't such a good idea. Try common sense, it may not seem as impressive, but it winds people up a lot less.

There is a skill to getting the balance of songs right. Ideally there will be some new ones, keeping the time fresh. This needs to be balanced by a sensitivity to not overdosing on new ones. It can be a killer to spend a worship time doing little more than trying to work out how each song goes. Probably it isn't sensible to start a worship time with a new song as it can sometimes set the tone for the meeting, encouraging people to watch rather than get involved. The second and third slots are good ones for new numbers, particularly if they can be repeated at the end.

So should there be a structure to a time of worship and are there biblical clues for song selection? In the Old Testament, we read how the Israelites worshipped in the temple. The temple was not only the place of gathering, it was also in a special way the place of God's presence. My friend, Mark Stibbe, has written a great book on the layout of the temple (*A Kingdom of Priests*, Darton Longman & Todd) and I want unashamedly to steal some bits from his book.

The temple design was intricately structured. As you entered through the gates, you came to the outer court. This was where the women would stay (sorry ladies, that's about as far as you got in those days). That was followed by the inner court which contained the holy place. There would be a veil between the inner court and what was called the most holy place, which is where the Ark of the Covenant was. It was here that God's manifest holy presence dwelt. It was such a holy place that only the chief priest could go in once a year in order to offer a sacrifice for the sins of the people.

Psalm 100 tells us to 'enter his gates with thanksgiving and his courts with praise', and it is a handy hint for the start of a worship set. Thanking God for the good things he has done was one of the distinctives of the Israelites. They were very good at reminding themselves of God's saving acts, keeping in mind the good things that he had done for them. When we begin worship with thanksgiving we are deciding to be grateful. We are reminding ourselves of some of the reasons for worship. When we 'count our blessings' we are led into the conscious knowledge of his presence.

Once through the gates and you're in the outer court, which was the place of praise. The root word of hallelujah (*hallel*) means praise, and points at the act of extolling God's character. It is saying, 'You're fantastic because you are kind, because you are good, because you are ever loving, your love is everlasting. You're powerful, you're majestic and glorious.' Consider a relationship: how much more intimate is it to praise someone for their good points than to thank them only for the things they have done? There is a dynamic to praise which none of us fully understands. I have been in many meetings where the atmosphere seemed at the beginning heavy and the meeting felt like we were wading through mud. Then we entered his courts with praise and after a while it was as if the spiritual clouds had lifted and we had broken through. Thanksgiving and praise are entry points to adoration and intimacy.

Things don't just stop there in the temple, as the holy place demands a new type of interaction. When we come to that place, words become almost superfluous. Sometimes you just need to rest in that place of

God's presence, and I have known times when I have been on my own before the Lord and everything around seems to have stopped. This is the place of two lovers just gazing into each other's eyes.

I think often, if we start with the gentle tender songs, we have to realise that people can come from all different sorts of places – they may have rushed in and could still be thinking about other things. Somehow we have got to give space for people to focus on God. People need to be brought into a place of intimacy rather than have it assumed that they are there already. Often worship leaders do not understand this dynamic. They have been praying and preparing for maybe two hours before the meeting so they are already in the place of intimacy when the meeting starts. They then become frustrated and discouraged when the congregation take a little longer to get there. The worship leader needs to lead them through the outer courts of thanksgiving and praise first.

Having progressed from the outer gates to the most holy place, the private place reserved for those who know how to be intimate with their God, it can be good to end up with songs of adoration, dedication or intercession. People often find it helpful to have a chance to say, 'Lord, I will do this task for you, what I have vowed I will make good.'

When selecting songs we also need to get the balance right between content and engagement. There are some songs (usually the more 'hymny' ones) which are packed full of scriptural truth but are quite difficult to engage with God through. At the other end of the spectrum there are songs ('Isn't he beautiful') which are tender and intimate (and even quite romantic in style) which, however, don't say very much. We need both. As any good nutritionist will tell you, we need a balanced diet. Too much content and the worship can become 'stodgy' and hard going. Not enough content and we can sometimes forget whom we are engaging with!

Having laid down all these general rules, it is good to remember that there are exceptions to every rule. Often the exception defines the rule, and sometimes the Holy Spirit may be doing something very different and the worship leader needs to go with that.

Choosing a Band

I feel fairly comfortable in suggesting that a seven-piece band for a midweek meeting in the front room is over the top. Considering exactly who will be in attendance at a meeting is hardly brain surgery, but the benefits are enormous. Deciding to ditch a load of drum and bass tunes will win you points with the congregation, should they be big fans of the 1662 service. The word is 'appropriate'.

When people like me write these things, there is often a tension between the ideal scenario and the harshness of reality. We've had plenty of musicians to choose from at Soul Survivor, and your choice may be more limited. It is important to remember to find your own balance between compromise and integrity.

First of all band members need to love the Lord and be worshippers. I know some say that it doesn't really matter if the rest of the band aren't worshipping as long as the worship leader is, but if a band are not united on this fundamental issue, how can they fully function as a band? Worship is a spiritual thing and these are spiritual principles we mustn't lose sight of.

At the same time the band members need to be as musically competent as possible. They need to work together well, there needs to be a humility and they need to defer to one another. The last thing you need in a time of worship is to have the lead guitarist and the keyboard player competing for solos, producing the sonic equivalent of a motorway pile-up. The worship leader needs to have the final responsibility for the music, and so needs to know a little bit about arrangements.

Many times the band will be more musical than the worship leader, and a good worship leader will make space for band members to be creative and make their suggestions. The leader bottom-lines the whole thing, and must keep it from becoming musically extravagant.

Before Leading, Read

Reading the words of the songs and having a good think about their meaning may not sound like a very groundbreaking suggestion, but it seems that many could do with taking the advice. It can be hard for a congregation to focus on their Creator when the songs they are singing have been chosen more for style than for content. Ideally, each song should follow on from its predecessor, building on certain themes that help the congregation do business with God. The results gained from such a selection will be noticeably better than from the set thrown together by the principle that the tunes are all quite nice. If we don't think about how songs link and where they fit in, we lose the sense of progression in our worship, that sense of moving closer towards the Lord.

Before Repeating, Think

Repetition is a big thing in worship. At times it's a good big thing, and at times it's a bad one. When singing one line for five minutes doesn't seem quite so anointed, I'll often wonder why the leader went for it. 'I felt led' seems to be the most common response, which I find puzzling; why would God lead you to do that? Does he hate us that much? No, sometimes feeling led is a euphemism for feeling stuck. Granted, certain songs contain bits that lend themselves to repetition. 'God Is Speaking Through the Music' is not one of them. I've been in meetings where the title line has been repeated thirty-two times. On lap seven I start to tire. Lap fourteen usually sees me begin to lose the ability to focus with my eyes. I'm dribbling by lap twenty and when we enter the home straight the battle to retain control of the last of my bodily functions is all but over. 'Stop,' I try to murmur with my last sane breath. 'Is there anyone here who *doesn't* know that God is speaking through the music?'

That song is a classic illustration of the gulf between satisfaction on stage and stupefaction in the seats: each time I have taken part in the 'God Is Speaking . . .' marathon, I've noticed that the same line that tortures me, manages to send the musos into twitching giblets of delight. Repetition should stem from a good reason, and should be carried out with care and restraint. If you want to repeat a song, have a reason in mind for doing so. Is there something new, which needs emphasising second time around? By varying the speed or musical accompaniment to the song, will it help to move from praise to adoration or vice versa?

In our church in Watford, we easily fell into the trap of stale unoriginality. We weren't repeating lines ad infinitum, but we were guilty of the same spirit of thoughtlessness. Each time of worship consisted of roughly ten songs, with each one being repeated three and a half times, with a double chorus added on at the end for good measure. You could set your watch by the songs (a boredom-avoiding tactic that many of the congregation employed).

But there is a danger in all this jovial mockery. First, we must avoid becoming consumers of worship: demanding a full refund if the service does not reach our high expectations. Second, we cannot deny the power of repetition. One of the reasons why the musicians always look so happy when they're doing a few circuits of 'God is Speaking . . .' is (apart from a sadistic enjoyment of congregational torture) that repetition can be good. They sit, so they tell me, in the 'groove'. I suppose, then, that the best worship leaders are those who can do just that: lead. The musicians' enjoyment of a certain moment can be an indication of its anointing, but it can also be their downfall, as leaders and their flock drift apart. The magic comes when the band on stage manage to take the people with them.

When Delirious? were called the Cutting Edge band they came to lead worship for the youth meetings at the New Wine festival. One particular evening things got a little interesting. Halfway through the worship, Martin Smith started singing his song 'I Could Sing of Your Love Forever'. He didn't get very far with it, as when the chorus came up, he simply repeated the title line of the song. Panic set in. I had been here before, and had only just recovered from a particularly vicious encounter with a multiple rendition of 'Isn't He Beautiful?' ('Isn't he?' we had asked, a lot). Had he got stuck, I wondered? Should I do the decent thing and go and offer to administer the Heimlich man-oeuvre to dislodge the offending syllable? Then I sensed that something was happening. All around the room, people were engaging with God. As the next twenty minutes progressed, the song didn't. We repeated the line over and over, and the effect was amazing. Some people were dropping to their knees; other people were crying; others were just standing there with their hands outstretched. And as I looked out it was like a bomb had hit the place. It was as though Jesus had walked in. Then the band just slowed it all down and did it with no instruments, then began building up to an almost screaming cres-cendo.

It has become my favourite example of how power-ful anointed repetition can be. Part was due, I suspect, to interplay between the words and our actions; we were singing of his love forever. It was magical, fresh and innovative. The danger would have been for Martin and the band to turn up to their next gig, pre-armed with a load of Cutting Edge repeats. It would have become a tradition, a technique. It may well have worked, but with each use the danger would have increased to view it as the ACME Instant Worship Success.

So far this whole bit with me cussing down repetition might have had you quietly fuming as you reach for Revelation and point to the bit about 'day and night they never stopped singing "Holy, holy, holy"'. I know and admit my argument might not be the tightest ever constructed. However, there's one large difference between the biblical examples and our terrestrial practices: Revelation is talking about heaven. God lives there and things are perfect. When we take things into our own hands down here, no matter how good our intentions are, we invariably end up producing a pale reflection of God's master plan.

Not that I'm down on music. There is a transcendent power within music that draws people towards it, and I would love to explore that relationship further. When the tones and mood are changed within a song, even in the most subtle of ways, they can open a door to God's presence. There's a recording of 'O Come Let Us Adore Him' that I like to listen to. It's simple, powerful and is capable of sending shivers down my spine. All that happens is the repetition of three phrases (O come let us adore him, for he alone is worthy, and we give you all the glory). Perhaps there is no real formula to getting the worship right. These guidelines may help manage the whole thing better, but at the end of the day, worship is about sacrifice, celebration, creation and dedication. It's up to each of us to keep it fresh – whether that 'it' might mean the music or our own attitudes.

Familiarity

If you know neither the words nor the tune, then probably, as a rule, it's worth putting the song on the metaphorical back burner. If not, the resulting humiliation may do your pride some good, but the congregation will suffer in the process. Few, we may think, would be stupid enough to actually play a song they didn't know, but you would be surprised. The distraction of hearing someone mess up a song completely is often enough to tear people away from focusing on Jesus. Straight away you come out of it thinking, 'He was singing the wrong line. What was he thinking of, how can he be worshipping if he doesn't even know the words?'

Before Stripping, Get Help

If you do feel a particular and specific calling to enter a time of prophetic singing, dancing, clapping or undressing, I would suggest that you do open your eyes at some stage to check that everyone else has not either left, fallen asleep, died or joined the Moonies. Again, I've given a small encouragement for us to pursue the goal of accessible worship. Not to say that accessible worship is code for nice, sensible, dull worship, just worship that doesn't require a degree-level familiarity with the subject.

The above is all common sense and it's amazing how often, in our desire to go deeper, we forget the simple things that make worship in song work. The temptation, especially if you've been leading worship for a while, is to consider that familiarity equates a lack of creativity. Instead of returning to the heart of worship, it is easy to subscribe to the idea that when things start to seem 'common', then it is up to the music to recapture the sense of wonder. It may well turn out that it is the music which receives an adrenaline boost, but it is to Jesus that we should first turn, rededicating our hearts and worship back to him. In all these things, there is one maxim I like to go by: KISS – Keep It Simple, Stupid.

Performance in Worship

It makes sense that the abilities that are associated with 'creative types' who perform in public transfer over to a worship context. To be a good worship leader is, among other things, to be able to create music that reflects God's own creativity. But if those skills and attributes work on both sides of the church doors, so too do the problems. You see, worship is not a performance, and God doesn't need entertaining, looking after or cheering up. We worship because it gives him his worth, something that is far too important to be contorted by our own egos and insecurities. And so we come to the perennial tension: if 'arty farties' tend to make good worship leaders (better, at least, than ex-accountants like myself), then how to avoid alienating and confusing the masses? Creatively challenging and dangerous it may be, but freestyle-Warholian-dub-worship-in-French probably would leave them confused at St Botolph's in the Marsh.

Performance often seems to be a main point of conflict between pastor and worship leader. I believe that worship is not about performance. A performing worship leader will distract attention from God and should be reminded that their role is to draw the congregation into the worship. That having been said, the example of David springs to mind. That whole dancing in a linen ephod thing was hardly shy, and we know for a fact that it got people's attention. However, when his wife criticised him, David's response was simple. 'I will celebrate before the Lord,' he said. David's only audience was his God. David's dance fell more into the 'exuberant and spontaneous act' category than in the one marked 'showing off'.

Some would say that it's unrealistic to tell a worship leader or a worship band to squash their performing instincts. They may also go on to suggest that speakers do their fair share of performing too, yet no one tells them to cut down on gags and tonal variation. I think that it is misleading to compare giving a talk with leading worship: the speaker imparts information, the worship leader ministers before the throne of heaven. No contest. Speakers need to attract attention to better their chances of getting their point across. The main aim of leading worship is not to impart information, it's to minister to God. First and foremost they are not even there to try and encourage the congregation to do the same: the first directive is to worship God themselves. If it happens that it is natural for someone to dance whenever they worship, then that's just fine. No one would call that sort of genuine expression a performance.

There is also a danger within this that, if you are a worship leader, you will finish reading this and step up to the mike at your next meeting looking as miserable as sin and staring at your feet. That too is a performance, my friend. Sorry. The truth is that we need to learn to be natural before God. It is not a question of trying to impress him, nor is it a chance for us to try and fool him. More than anything, it is a chance to be genuine before him.

This is not an oh-so-subtle way of me declaring my hatred of performance music (look through my CD collection and you will see plenty of recordings by the king of rock performance – the mighty Meatloaf). I'm thrilled with the way that many have taken music from the church out into the charts, and I am not advocating that we become boring and uneventful so that nobody will want to watch us. We just need to make sure that we are being appropriate. The best worship leaders lead strongly and visibly enough that people will follow, but not so strongly that they themselves become the focus. While the prime directive for the leader is to worship God themselves, they must not forget their second aim, which is to encourage others to follow. They are not there to create observers, but to ignite and direct others. The Church has struggled for long enough to get people involved, and the last thing we need to be doing now is to create observers.

Accessibility

Lately there has been a fairly lively debate going on about how complicated our worship should be. The discussions focus on the nature of the music, and are a reflection of the way that worship music has developed over recent years. As more time and resources have been directed towards the 'industry', so there has been a pursuit of quality, particularly in relation to many of the albums that are recorded. Magazines now produce charts of the most popular songs, which themselves are increasingly influenced by mainstream music tastes. Alongside the debate is the feeling on the ground; for some people, many of these new songs are unbearably naff. A classically trained organist at a church I belonged to refused to play modern worship music as he found it so musically retarded. At the other extreme, it doesn't take much in the way of imagination to envisage a bunch of teenage punks rejecting the comfortable sweaters and rainbow guitar straps of contemporary worship music. Let's be honest, much of what comes out of the worship scene bears more than a passing resemblance to Retro Folk.

While I'm too scared of the classically trained organist, I do feel that I have a few things to say about the attitude that bemoans the lack of musical innovation in church. One of the things that musicians tend to do (apart from sleep) is to want to experiment. When something new is being created, something that pushes against the boundaries of experience, then two things happen. First, the musos get very happy. Second, the congregation leave. Because innovation can mean so much to the band, it often becomes inaccessible to those whom they are supposed to be leading. Surely, for leaders, accessibility should rank as highly on the Most Wanted list as skill, creativity and the ability to drift off into space at a moment's notice?

I'll never forget how Kevin Prosch recently led worship at a Soul Survivor festival for an hour without singing one song. It was prophetic and intense. Kevin blew his horns, hit his ethnic percussive instruments and sang spontaneous refrains. The response amongst the musicians and those with their A Levels in Worship was phenomenal. For many, it was without doubt the best time of worship they had ever experienced. However, nearly 10 per cent of the congregation left the hall, scratching their heads and wondering what on earth it was all about. At the time I was confused too. How had so many been so blessed, at the same time that so many had been put off?

After much thought I came up with the following three conclusions:

1. Liturgy is important. I'm not talking about specific liturgy here, just the concept of having a structure for saying something through the worship time. We need to make sure that our services are Christ-centred, that he is at the very heart of them. We need to sing about Jesus as well as to him, and we need to focus on the single most significant act in the history of the universe (his death upon the cross, if you're wondering). These are vital ingredients as without them there is little more than the music for the people to catch onto. Having said that there also needs to be time and place for spontaneity, for silence, for music without words, but it has to be in the context of people expressing their own worship of God. That will be hard to do if they have spent the previous forty-five minutes wondering what sort of socks the person in front is wearing.

2. Whilst this particular time at Soul Survivor was great for the musos, the non-musicians felt marginalised and excluded. Perhaps there are times when the worship leader needs to hold back – perhaps not

so much that they play to the lowest common denominator – just enough to encourage the people to follow. As the overall leader of the meeting I should have explained and given a reference point for what was going to happen beforehand.

3. I have to deliver some bad news: the music is not the meat in the worship sandwich; it's the napkin that helps you not to get your jumper dirty. Music is a tool, not the goal.

The Songwriter and the Bible

One of the exciting things that seems to be happening lately is new songs are being written that contain fresh ways of expressing the eternal truths. At times it seems as though new songs turn up each week, and the key to their success appears to be the extent to which they are rooted in Scripture.

Someone said that a good worship song is a song with a universal theme put in a unique way. One or two of our worship songs have been very unique, although slightly lacking when it comes down to universality. Some of them have been very personal songs, relating powerfully to the lives of the writer or a select few, but failing to impact the wider Church. As a rule of thumb, taking the thematic direction straight from the Bible guarantees that the song will be both accessible and theologically correct.

The Leader

The role of the worship leader is to act in the same way as an Old Testament priest. Thankfully that does not

125

mean going as far as the home-spun robes and ques-
tionable personal hygiene, but it does involve representing the people to the Lord and the Lord to the
people. Worship leaders need to be asking the Lord
regularly for direction. 'Lord, what are you wanting to
say to the people?' might be one thought that is on
their mind during the week. They also need to stay
close to the rest of the church so they have a sense of
what is already going on in people's lives.

If the worship leader only ever worships with eyes
closed it sends a message out to the congregation that
it is the leader alone who can commune with God.
That can be arrogant. The Holy Spirit can lead the
worship through the whole congregation and sometimes if the worship leader is not in tune with them, he
or she misses what the Holy Spirit is starting to stir up
in the congregation. For example, it may be that the
Holy Spirit is moving in the congregation so that a
number seem spontaneously to go to their knees in a
sign of reverence and brokenness. Miss that and go
into a turbo-charged version of 'Joy Is the Flag' and
some of the magic is gone.

Musical Ability and Anointing

Whilst musical ability is important, it is not the first
thing that one is looking for in a worship leader or a
worship band. The most important attribute is a
desire to be a worshipper. Great skill alone won't
be enough, it can turn heads and hearts, but to draw
people into God's presence needs something special:
anointing. In one sense, anointing is one of those
strange things that you know when it's there and you

know when it's not, but is very hard to define. Having said that, let's have a little go.

The word anointed comes from the Hebrew word for Messiah. The Greek word that is used for Christ throughout the New Testament translates as anointed one. So to be anointed means to have something of the Messiah, something of Christ, something of heaven. You know when a worship time is anointed as there is a sense of the presence of Jesus there, the glory of God, the activity of the Holy Spirit. When the anointing is around there is a real sense of both excitement and unpredictability in the place. That's what we should all be praying and yearning for.

But how do you get the anointing? Certainly it seems to co-exist with prayer, and when a congregation come together with a common desire to worship and give to God, there often seems to be something special about the worship that follows. It reminds me of the verse in Psalm 22 that says 'the Lord inhabits the praises of his people'. God's anointed presence is more likely to come when hearts are ready rather than far from him. So anointing has something to do with expectancy, something to do with being prepared to give in worship.

The logical progression from this is that if the congregation is obeying the Lord in the week and worshipping him through times on their own, the anointing will come. Kevin Prosch has said that the anointing rides on faithfulness. Although God's blessings cannot be turned on like a tap, I'm sure that choosing to follow a lifestyle that disobeys God's commands is not the best way of inviting God's presence. Thankfully, however, God is a good deal more gracious than we are, and he throws into the mix things like grace and compassion, bestowing his anointing wherever he sees fit.

Does that mean that the times that feel like wading through porridge are worthless? If it isn't all fizz and sparkle wouldn't it have been better if we had stayed at home and watched *Star Trek*? Far from being wasted, those are the times when God is calling us to put some effort into finding him for ourselves. There is a passage in the book of Song of Songs where the lover comes bounding over the hills and approaches the house of his beloved. He doesn't go inside, though, and chooses to look in through the window for a while before leaving. Instead of forgetting his key or suddenly coming over all shy, the lover is beckoning the beloved to come out of the house and join him. Sometimes the Lord doesn't come right into our house, he calls us to go and pursue him, to seek after him.

The Secret Place

A worship leader needs to work hard at worshipping the Lord on his or her own. Matt and I used to meet together on a Saturday night and worship the Lord, and over time we both grew in our relationship with God. There are plenty of worship leaders out there waiting for their 'big break' to come along, holding off on putting in some hard work until they see the rewards around the corner. This conflicts with the biblical principle of God looking for people who are faithful in small things before he gives them a chance to be faithful in the big things.

This is exactly the way that it happened with David. When he was anointed by Samuel he was just a child, yet he was being told by the prophet that he would one day be King of Israel. He didn't see the fulfilment of that prophecy for many years, and from Scripture it doesn't even look as though he got any time off to celebrate his good fortune (in Samuel 17 it says that he went back to look after the sheep). I think it was while he was looking after the sheep that he learned to be a worship leader. It was isolated, lonely and very humble, with none around to see what he was up to. Psalm 23 ('The Lord is my shepherd, I shall not want. He makes me lie down in green pastures . . .') is definitely one for the 'Best Of' compilation of his work, and is saturated with imagery relating to the life of a shepherd. I suspect it was written in that environment, that secret place.

I believe this is a key lesson that Christians need to learn. In our activist Christianity we are often doing things all the time, existing in a continual state of achieving. We need to learn that the heart of the Christian faith is relationship with Jesus, and the way that God has chosen for us to express relationship with him is through worship. A. W. Tozer once said, 'Worship is the missing jewel of the church.' How right he was.

To learn to minister to the Lord when no one else is there is preparation for ministering to the Lord when thousands of people are there. Whatever the occasion we must always act as if we're worshipping solely for an audience of one. It shouldn't matter if there are just three people or three thousand, because the most important audience is the One in heaven.

The Magic Formula

Sometimes things go right. When that happens the best course of action is not to record every minute detail of the session in the hope that it can all be repeated again next week. Unfortunately it doesn't quite work like that, and God seems to like to keep us on our toes (or knees, to be precise).

The Israelites encountered this eternal truth while wandering in the desert. When they realised that they had neither food nor water, they started complaining. Moses was the lucky recipient of their griping, and so he went to the Lord and asked him for some help. By return the Lord told him to strike a nearby rock and water would come out. Moses did as he was told and everyone had a drink. God had showed up and everyone was happy and wet (Exodus 17:1–7).

A little while later and they're in the same position – thirsty (see Numbers 20). Again Moses got it in the neck, and again he went off and asked God what to do. This time around the Lord said, 'Moses, go to this rock and speak to it and you will see what happens.' So Moses went to the rock in front of the people but this time he didn't speak to it as he was told, he struck it, as he had the time before. Now this is very interesting because water came out and in that sense it still 'worked', but it wasn't the same. The Lord was displeased with Moses and he told him that because of that he wouldn't enter the Promised Land. We will never know the answer to the question, what would have happened if Moses had spoken to the rock and not struck it?

2. *How to Sort It Out When It All Goes Wrong*

So your church is full of musos with the expertise of Lenny Kravitz and the spiritual maturity of the Apostle Paul. Your fellow congregation members have all happily moved on from Tambourine Praise to something slightly more funky, turning your meetings into multifaceted expressions of unity, worship and truth. Things are going so well that people are even finding lyrical inspiration in the book of Kings. In short, you're all flying, and you're not even getting proud about it. But there's a problem: something's not quite right. Try as hard as you might, you just can't seem to get it together, so what do you do about it?

First up it's time to relax. Worship is one of those things that sometimes is hard work for no apparent reason. As we have seen, the whole idea of a magic formula is a red herring, although there are still plenty of things we can do about it. Instead of denouncing it all as irrelevant and leaving the church, take time out to consider the following and see where you end up.

We've already mentioned the story of the lover in the Song of Songs, and are familiar with the idea that there are times when God simply hides his face from us in order that we might chase after him a little more earnestly. These might be some of the few times when he can teach us about perseverance, but we shouldn't be too quick to point the finger in God's direction every time the fizz seems to have subsided. Much of the time it is worth looking into our own lives to see if we might find the root of our dissatisfaction within.

131

I'm sorry if this comes as a surprise, but it can be our fault.

Reasons

If you're not spending time with the Lord throughout the week I'm afraid that it is going to be impossible to come to church on a Sunday and try suddenly to switch on a relationship. If we have defined worship as a relationship, then this idea stands to reason. You can't have a marriage like that, and you certainly cannot use ninety minutes of interaction per week as a solid basis for a friendship with God. Worship and the relationship that surrounds it is not something you can switch on and off. Instead, it is my responsibility to talk to the Lord, to worship him and to read his Word regularly, otherwise when I come with others to worship there is nothing there but empty words.

While we're on this point, there can often be hindrances when we hide sin in our hearts. Now everybody sins, but when we know what's true, when we are aware of the things that God has commanded, yet we have chosen to disobey God, then we can end up in trouble. It's very difficult to be indulging in habitual sins during the week and then to try and forget about them when you turn up at church.

It can be confusing at times when we consider the nature of contemporary worship. On the surface it seems as though people are doing everything they can to make sure that the sessions are attractive, accessible and easy to follow. It can almost seem that this is done to make it easy for us, just like a trip to the cinema. Unfortunately, while it is important to make it easier for us to join in, we cannot abdicate all responsibility. Remember that bit about sacrifice? Sometimes we forget that worship is primarily a sacrifice. Our culture of immediate gratification has virtually crash landed our boredom thresholds and left us petulant and lazy. As the saying goes, worship is 'our duty and our joy'.

We went through a similar situation at Soul Survivor Watford. With a spanking new building, a congregation wearing combat trousers and links with the booming summer festivals, some might have thought that we had it sussed. Beneath the surface though, there have been continual struggles to keep on track and not get distracted. By Easter 1997 the church was in a rut and needed immediate attention.

Since it began – meeting in school halls with a PA that packed into the boot of a Cavalier – we have always given plenty of time over to worshipping through music. Over the years people have poured out their hearts to God through it, and we've seen people healed, changed and set free during many of the worship times.

We began to get a bit confused at the beginning of 1997. On the surface everything was just fine – many of the musicians had worked out how to tune their instruments and the sound engineers were getting out of bed on time – and each service contained a block of songs that focused on the cross and gave people the chance to get down to business with God. To make this easier the music was (nearly) up to date, the chairs had disappeared and the lights were low. What better atmosphere for people to relax?

But that was the problem: people weren't relaxed.

Instead of focusing solely on God, the whole thing had become so cluttered, so concerned with details that everyone in the church – leaders and congregation alike – became distracted by the worship. Was it Redman's fault? I listened . . . he wasn't singing any more duff notes than usual. Then it clicked. We had become connoisseurs of worship instead of participants in it. In our hearts we marked the worship out of ten: 'Not that song again', 'I can't hear the bass', 'I like the way she sings'. It was as if the outcome of the session depended on the people who were up on the stage, as if they were responsible for making it a good or bad time of worship. Although it never quite reached this stage, at times it felt as if you could switch off if someone played something you didn't like.

We were challenged to ask ourselves individually, 'When I come through the door of the church, what am I bringing as my contribution to the worship?' Then the truth came to us: worship is not a spectator sport, it is not a product moulded by the taste of the consumers. It is not about what we can get out of it. It is all about God.

We needed to take drastic action. So we banned the band. The big meeting room was closed off and the lights turned up. For a couple of months the church services were totally different: nobody led worship – if someone wanted to sing they started a song. If not, we would have silence. We agreed that if no one brought a sacrifice of praise we would spend the meeting in silence. At the beginning we virtually did! It was a very painful process. We were learning again not to rely on the music. After a while we began to have some very sweet times of worship. We all began to bring our prayers, our readings, our prophecies, our thanksgiving, our praises and our songs. Someone would start a song a capella and we would all join in. Then someone else would take it on with another song. The excitement came back. We were once again meeting with God. With all the comforts stripped away people worshipped from the heart.

When we had learnt our lesson, we brought the band back. It was at this point that Matt began to sing the song he had written out of this experience, 'The Heart of Worship'. The words express exactly what was going on:

When the music fades,
All is stripped away, and I simply come,
Longing just to bring
Something that's of worth
That will bless your heart.

I'll bring you more than a song,
For a song in itself is not what you have required.
You search much deeper within,
Through the way things appear;
You're looking into my heart.

I'm coming back to the heart of worship,
And it's all about you,
All about you, Jesus.
I'm sorry, Lord, for the thing I've made it,
When it's all about you,
All about you, Jesus.

King of endless worth
No one could express
How much you deserve.
Though I'm weak and poor
All I have is yours, every single breath.

Matt Redman
Copyright 1997 Kingsway's
Thankyou Music/MCPS

Another reason our worship goes stale is that we simply have lost the wonder of our salvation. The joy of it all has gone out the window as we have forgotten exactly how much we have been forgiven. Jesus said once that he who is forgiven much loves much and yet he who is forgiven little loves little. In other words, if we realise how much we have been forgiven and what forgiveness means, our response will be great in our worship. But unfortunately, some of us can forget, and we end up fooling ourselves that we aren't that bad after all. When we see the cross, when we remember what Jesus did for our forgiveness, then we begin to recapture that sense of wonder.

When we don't hear God's voice we struggle to enjoy our relationship with him. In 1 Samuel 2 we find a description of a time when the words of the Lord were rare in Israel. There are times when we also go through a quiet patch, and at first glance the situation is drastic. After all, how do you chase up a missing deity? Thankfully that's exactly why we have the Bible, so that we can constantly be hearing his voice. If as a church we are not getting stuck into the Scriptures, then we will be missing out on much of God's input into our relationship with him.

If we are all mouth and no trousers, blaggers instead of doers, then the chances are that we will be going through a bit of a dry patch in the worship too. Christianity is a multi-dimension way of life; and like cells, each is dependent on the other. If we are failing to obey Jesus's commands about going after the lost sheep then we will be missing out on an important aspect of our faith. Sometimes we can become very self-indulgent, turning up at church expecting to be fed all the time. I have heard countless individuals say that they need more teaching, more meat for them to get their spiritual molars into. I love John Wimber's response to the same situation; he said, 'The meat is on the streets.' Jesus's food was to obey God and proclaim his word. Likewise we have clear directives regarding our own lives. The greatest boost to worship is effective evangelism, and when we are out there with our neighbours, proclaiming Jesus in our lives and words, then we will be able to enjoy a fuller relationship with God. Also, there is nothing quite like seeing people saved to inspire praise and worship.

Carrying on from this idea of having a lack of balance within our lives, we can also get into trouble when we try and worship without being involved in issues of social justice and caring for the poor. One of the things that we have been learning at Soul Survivor over the last few years is that you cannot separate worship and justice in the Bible. The worship of God is also to care for the unfortunate, the broken, the hurting, the poor and the weak. If we are not doing that, if we're not actively involved in social concern and caring for others, then our worship is meaningless. In Amos 5 the Lord says, 'I hate, I despise your religious feasts; I cannot stand your assemblies . . . Away with the noise of your songs! . . . But let justice roll down like a river, righteousness like a never-failing stream!' (vv. 21, 23, 24). In Isaiah 58 God sends a message through the prophet to the people of Israel. They were fasting for one day in the belief that it would be enough to secure God's protection. God told them that the fast he has chosen is 'to loose the chains of injustice and to set the oppressed free'. It is 'to share your food with the hungry and to provide the poor wanderer with shelter – when you see the naked, to clothe him' (vv. 6, 7). True fasting, like true worship, involves caring for the poor and seeking justice. If this is not on the menu, then our ministry to the Lord when we come together is less than he requires.

Juicy Quotes on Worship

John Wimber: 'The difficulty will not be so much in the writing of new and great music; the test will be the godliness of those who deliver it . . .'

Graham Kendrick: 'As people like Balaam and Saul demonstrate, anointing does not guarantee godly character and right motives. In fact, it tests them to the extreme.'

G.K. Chesterton: 'Sometimes our religion is "more a theory than a love affair".'

Christina Rossetti: 'Heaven is revealed to earth as the homeland of music' – commenting on Revelation 4 and 5.

Henry Blackaby: 'Don't just do something, stand there!'

William Booth: 'Music is to the soul what wind is to the ship, blowing her onwards in the direction in which she is already steered.'

Oswald Chambers: 'The consequence of abandonment never enters into our outlook because our life is so taken up with Him.'

John Wimber: 'Historically every move of God has produced new music. Sometimes the music actually precipitated revival, sometimes it occurred during revival, but it was always present in the aftermath . . .'

John Wimber: 'Think about it; if worship leads every move of God, as it did in the Old Testament, where do you think the enemy will attack? And do you think he will have mercy and not attack at the point of weakness? If you think that you don't know anything about him and you don't know anything about the art of warfare.'

Kevin Prosch: 'The anointing rides on faithfulness.'

Oswald Chambers: 'Complete weakness and dependence will always be the occasion for the Spirit of God to manifest His power.'

William Cowper: 'Where is the blessedness I knew when I first saw the Lord? Where is the soul-refreshing view of Jesus and His word?'

Dietrich Bonhoeffer: 'When Christ calls a man, he bids him come and die.'

Charles Wesley: 'Let earth no more my heart divide, with Christ may I be crucified.'

Oswald Chambers: 'How can we talk of making a sacrifice for the Son of God? Our salvation is from hell and perdition and we talk about making sacrifices?'

Anglican liturgy: 'That we may show forth your praise not only with our lips but also with our lives.'

Charles R. Swindoll: 'The very best proof of your love for God is obedience – nothing more, nothing less, nothing else.'

A.W. Tozer: 'Out of enraptured, admiring, adoring, worshipping souls God does his work. The work done by a worshipper will have eternity in it.'

Former Archbishop of Canterbury, William Temple: 'To worship is to quicken the conscience by the holiness of God, to feed the mind with the truth of God, to purge the imagination by the beauty of God, to devote the will to the purpose of God.'

Brother Lawrence: 'I made this resolution to give myself wholly to God as the very best return I could make to him for his love. Because of my love for God, I then renounce all.'

John Piper: 'Worship is a way of gladly reflecting back to God the radiance of his worth.'

Graham Kendrick wrote that the priority of worship must be to give 'pleasure and glory to the One who is the subject of our worship'.

A.W. Tozer: 'True worship is to be so personally and hopelessly in love with God, that the idea of a transfer of affection never even remotely exists.'

Louie Giglio: 'Worship is a participation sport in a spectator culture.'

Postscript

This book carries the title *For the Audience of One* for the simple reason that when it comes to worship, it is God alone who is the audience. But there's a problem with this idea, as I have recently been discovering. In saying that we are the performers and that God is the audience, we give the impression that it is up to God to applaud our efforts. It turns the natural order of things upside down by implying that we deserve something back for all the hard work we put into the performance. Worst of all, it puts us at the heart of worship. Actually God is at the heart of worship, and when we worship, we are the ones who make up the audience, offering our songs and our lives in response to the wonders he has performed. Worship is our applause, our ovation to the God who is brilliant, who does such fantastic things and who has shown himself supremely in the face of his Son. The Lion who became a lamb, the King who became a servant, the Creator who became a Saviour.